THRILLS, CHILLS & SPILLS

THRILLS, CHILLS & SPILLS

A PHOTOGRAPHIC HISTORY
OF EARLY AVIATION
ON THE WORLD'S MOST BIZARRE AIRPORT —
THE BEACH AT DAYTONA BEACH, FLORIDA
1906 – 1929

DICK & YVONNE PUNNETT

PUBLISHED BY
LUTHERS
NEW SMYRNA BEACH, FLORIDA

Published by
LUTHERS
1009 North Dixie Freeway
New Smyrna Beach, FL 32618-6221

PRINTED IN THE UNITED STATES OF AMERICA

LIBRARY OF CONGRESS CATALOGING-IN-PUBLICATION DATA
Punnett, Dick, 1924-
Thrills, chills & spills : a photographic history of early
aviation on the world's most bizzare airport — the beach at Daytona
Beach, Florida, 1906-1929 / Dick & Yvonne Punnett.
p. cm.
Includes bibliographical references and index.
ISBN 1-877633-10-0 (hc) — ISBN 1-877633-09-7 (pbk.) : $17.95
1. Aeronautics — United States — History. 2. Airports — Florida —
Daytona Beach — History. I. Punnett, Yvonne, 1930- . II. Title.
III. Title: Thrills, chills, and spills.
TL521.P84 1990
629.13'00973—dc20   90-42545
                                                                      CIP

This book is dedicated
to Barbara Lindley Mason
in memory of her father, William Lindley,
who typified the spirit, enthusiasm and individualism
of early aviators during the barnstorming era of the twenties.

ACKNOWLEDGMENTS

The writing of this book has placed us under many obligations pleasant to record. Our first debt is to Elizabeth Baker, Executive Secretary of the Halifax Historical Society, Daytona Beach, Florida, whose unstinting cooperation and support really made this book possible.

We owe a very large debt to Barbara Lindley Mason, whose generosity in sharing her late father's collection of photographs and clippings filled many huge gaps in our narrative.

We are indebted to Steve Pappas for allowing us access to *The News-Journal* Library, and to General Kenneth L. Tallman for his permission to obtain photographic copies of illustrations from the Special Collections at the Embry-Riddle Aeronautical University Library.

In the long list of others who have aided us with pictures and/or materials in various ways, we wish especially to thank in alphabetical order the following people:

Harding Ballough, Daytona Beach, Florida
Herbert Budgen, Daytona Beach, Florida
William J. Dreggors, Jr., DeLand, Florida
Mrs. Gustav Ekstrom, Coral Gables, Florida
Dr. Paul E. Garber, Historian Emeritus & Ramsey Fellow,
   National Air & Space Museum, Smithsonian Institution,
   Washington, D.C.
John Gontner, Daytona Beach, Florida
Edwina Hallman, Boston, Georgia
Carol Harris, Curator, The Florida Room,
   Haydon Burns Public Library, Jacksonville, Florida
Floyd Herrick, Daytona Beach, Florida
John P. Ingle, Jr., Jacksonville, Florida
Stanton Kluge, Macon, Georgia

Edward McGowan, Gainesville, Georgia
Glenn E. Messer, Birmingham, Alabama
Dorothy Miller, Jacksonville, Florida
Vivian Robinson, Port Orange, Florida
James Tillis, DeLand, Florida

Without the generous cooperation of the following libraries and other institutions, we would not have had access to photographs or information invaluable to this book:

Birthplace of Speed Museum, Ormond Beach, Florida
The News-Journal Library, Daytona Beach, Florida
Embry-Riddle Aeronautical University Library,
   Daytona Beach, Florida
Florida State Archives Photographic Collection,
   Florida Department of State, Tallahassee, Florida
University of Florida, P.K. Yonge Library of Florida,
   Gainesville, Florida
The Glenn H. Curtiss Museum of Local History,
   Hammondsport, New York
Halifax Historical Society, Daytona Beach, Florida
Haydon Burns Public Library, Jacksonville, Florida
National Air & Space Museum Research Library,
   Smithsonian Institution, Washington, D.C.
National Automotive History Collection,
   Detroit Public Library, Detroit, Michigan
Princeton University Archives, Princeton, New Jersey
Rochester Central Library, Rochester, New York
St. Augustine Historical Society, St. Augustine, Florida

Special appreciation is expressed to Gary Luther, New Smyrna Beach, Florida, for his photographic copying expertise, and to Jean Lewis for proofreading our manuscript.

TABLE OF CONTENTS

Photographer: Richard H. LeSesne

Daytona Beach, Florida

INTRODUCTION

The idea of an airport on an ocean beach seems totally impractical. What about tides? Or crosswinds? What about the people who use the beach — the bathers, the sun tan crowd, or the strollers? Certainly a beach is no place for airplanes with their big whirling propellers! And yet, on Daytona's beach in the pioneer days of aviation all of these factors were adjusted to by pilots and their aircraft, and sometimes with very odd results!

After all, there were obvious advantages to having an airport on a beach. For one thing, the beach was nature-made and therefore free. Furthermore, speaking specifically of the beach at Daytona, all the amenities existed a few feet in back of the ocean dunes. Two towns (Daytona Beach and Seabreeze) and several hotels lined the beach. No need to locate an airport on the outskirts of town in the nearest available large field. The beach airport, in effect, was located downtown!

Small wonder, then, that this airport really did exist and was used every year from 1911 to the early 1940's. Yet, in spite of the odd nature of this airport and the bizarre things that happened on it, the memory of it has all but disappeared. It might have remained that way, except for a Daytona Beach amateur photographer and collector named Lawson Diggett. When he died, he left all of his photographs to the Halifax Historical Society. It is a lively picture record of the area, especially the beach. His numerous photographs of aviation activities on the beach amazed and inspired the authors, and led to the idea for this book.

During the development of this book it became apparent that as a by-product the book was also a celebration of the year 1903. In that year two public discoveries provided the impetus for our story. The most important discovery occurred on December 17, 1903, when Wilbur and Orville Wright conclusively proved that man could fly. With Orville at the controls, their primitive aircraft lifted from the remote dunes of Kitty Hawk, North Carolina, and made the first engine-powered flight of a heavier-than-air machine. By the end of that same day the Wrights had made three more flights, with the two brothers taking turns at flying the machine. The air age had begun.

Ironically, those epocal flights went almost unnoticed by the press, while earlier that same year a lesser event made newspapers all over the country. In January 1903 the country discovered a great natural racecourse when the first annual automobile races and speed trials were held on the wide, hard sands of the Ormond-Daytona beach. This book chronicles how the two discoveries coalesced into a colorful, little known chapter in American aviation history.

After the realization that the Ormond-Daytona beach was a natural racecourse for automobiles, it was a simple step to the perception that the beach was also a natural airport! Specifically, it was an airport with a runway 300 to 500 feet wide at low tide that ran in a straight line for over 25 miles. This magnificent beach runway was also as smooth as a table top and almost as hard as cement. Furthermore, it was maintenance free. The beach was swept clean by a tidal broom twice a day!

There aren't many other places in the United States where airplanes have consistently and safely landed and taken off from a beach. The only place we know of other than the northeast coast of Florida is Old Orchard Beach in Maine. A local pilot named Harry Jones used to fly from there occasionally, and at least five transatlantic flights started from there during the twenties and thirties.

But for consistent flying, day in and day out, over a period of many years, with hangars and airplane service included, there was really only one beach — Daytona Beach. And now it's all but forgotten. That's the reason for writing this book — to recall a bizarre chapter in American aviation history, a time when automobiles, bathers, bicycles, horse and buggies, tourists and airplanes all shared the same wide, hard stretch of sand!

The Ludlow glider encounters a gust of wind as it is positioned for a towed flight on Ormond Beach in 1906. Pilot Charles K. Hamilton can be seen sitting in a web of rope on the lower plane of the glider.

THE EARLY BIRDS

Photo Courtesy National Automotive History Collection, Detroit Public Library

**Volunteers move the Ludlow glider into position for
Florida's first glider flight.**

Looking very much like the world's largest box kite, the contraption shown above was actually a glider. It was designed and built by Israel Ludlow, a prominent New York lawyer and amateur scientist. Ludlow was using his gliders to study flight characteristics of a heavier-than-air machine, but on this occasion he sent the glider to Ormond Beach as an added attraction during the 1906 auto races. The flight of this glider became the first aviation event on the beach.

The man Ludlow sent to pilot the glider was a diminutive, and very jug-eared, redhead named Charles K. Hamilton. Hamilton was already famous as an aerial daredevil, having made several flights in Ludlow's gliders. During those flights he was towed aloft kite-fashion by boat or automobile, after which he released the tow rope for an extended glide back to

earth. To assess just how dangerous these flights were, consider the experience of World War II glider pilots more than 35 years later. Even with advanced equipment, they found towed flight a very tricky and dangerous business when they were developing large personnel gliders for transporting infantry.

In Hamilton's time the problem of towed flights was compounded by very primitive control methods. He stood between upper and lower wings on a precarious platform which was nothing more than a flimsy web of rope. Holding on to the thin bamboo framework, he tried to control the flight by a rapid and perhaps frantic shifting of his weight.

Small wonder that on the day he flew, January 17, 1906, the entire town of Ormond closed up shop and lined the beach to watch!

Hamilton was towed aloft by auto, but the flight only went about 150 feet before a wing rib broke and a minor crash occurred. Hamilton, who was unhurt, had at least gained the distinction of being the first aviator to make a takeoff and landing on the beach. And it was the first flight in Florida of a glider towed by an automobile.

After the minor crash, the Ludlow glider was easily repaired, being constructed of bamboo and silk. Several days later Hamilton tried another towed flight. This time he achieved a height of 250 feet, erratically climbing and diving down the beach before finally plunging in a half circle and colliding with a flagpole just north of the Bretton Inn. Hamilton was thrown onto a boardwalk but bounced up with nothing worse than a bruised knee!

On the left the figure of Hamilton is dwarfed by the huge kite as he shifts his weight to correct the dipping right wings.

Here is the great pioneer pilot himself — Charles Keeney Hamilton. With those amazing outstretched ears, one might almost expect him to fly all by himself!

The picture on the left was taken just after the crash. Note the offending flagpole still standing intact. Also note the webbed platform seen in about the middle of the kite.

Hamilton's second crash ended his flights at Ormond. In the early spring of 1906 he took the Ludlow glider to Jacksonville Beach and rendezvoused with Ludlow. Unwisely, Ludlow elected to take the place of the indestructible Hamilton and pilot the glider himself. Shortly after being towed aloft he crashed, sustaining injuries that confined him to a wheelchair for the rest of his life.

Hamilton went on to become one of the great pioneers of manned flight. He learned to fly motor-driven aircraft and was the twelfth man to receive an American pilot's license.

At the end of his career he had crashed a total of 63 times! Even so, he was considered one of the most skillful of the early fliers, and eventually died in bed, just as he had predicted all along. But there's a catch. The crashes had taken their toll, and he died of an internal hemorrhage on January 22, 1914. He was only 32.

On the left is the first engine-propelled heavier-than-air machine to appear on Daytona Beach. As was typical of some of the early aircraft designs, it's hard to tell the front from the rear! In this case the aircraft faces the ocean.

Photo Courtesy Herbert Budgen

Three years after Hamilton's glider flights, the strange contraption illustrated on this page was brought to Daytona Beach by Carl Bates. It was built by Bates and two other men, all of them from Chicago, Illinois. It featured a 10-hp engine of Bates' own design, and critics remarked that the aircraft was underpowered and wouldn't fly. Bates brought the airplane to the beach in 1909 as an attraction during the March automobile races, but heavy winds kept postponing any flight attempts. Finally the winds abated and a large crowd gathered on the beach to watch what would be the first engine-propelled flight in Florida. The engine started smoothly and the aircraft ran on its wheels down the beach, but failed to take off. Undaunted, Bates tried again a few days later.

Here's his account of what happened in *Aeronautics* magazine for April 1909:

"Everyone seemed to doubt my ability to get off the ground...and would not accept my invitation to come over to the beach to see me try once more. However, I managed to get a few loyal enthusiasts to help me try the machine on the morning of the 29th of March, and on this occasion I made a flight of 460 yards, a little over a quarter mile. This was my first real flight and the only one I ever made with my machine. I would have flown further if the flywheel had held longer, but it suddenly came loose again, setting up a terrific vibration, which caused the propeller to break loose and shatter the ribs and main rear timbers of the aeroplane; however, the machine landed easily without further damage. The fellows with me at the time said the machine was on the average about 10 to 12 feet above the ground, but on one occasion rose as high as 20 feet or more."

Did Bates really fly? No one can be sure. He never submitted to the Aero Club of America the required number of corroborating statements from witnesses.

If he had, he would be credited with the first airplane flight in Florida. Instead, that honor went to Lincoln Beachey, who flew in Orlando in February 1910.

Photo Courtesy Birthplace of Speed Museum

This is probably the beginning of the race that never was! Carl Bates and his airplane are matched against Louis Strang in his Buick racer sometime during the auto races in March 1909. It seems likely that local photographer R.H. LeSesne staged this scene, because the local newspapers of the day make no mention of such a contest.

Strang might have caught the flying bug from Bates. He decided to quit race car driving and become a pilot. But when he observed the high casualty rate of pioneer fliers and had some close calls of his own during flight training, he promptly switched back to the relative safety of auto racing!

Photo Courtesy Halifax Historical Society

This is the only known photograph of the first twin-engine airplane ever built and flown anywhere in the world. Copied from an old stereograph, it makes its first published appearance in this book.

The photograph on the facing page was taken on Daytona Beach sometime in the first half of 1910, just prior to the aircraft's initial test flight. This first twin-engine plane was designed and built by Edward F. Andrews, a resident of Chicago who wintered in Daytona.

No identification of individuals appeared on the stereograph; so the gent in the vest and wearing the straw hat may or may not be Andrews. His design was a biplane powered by two 36-hp Adams-Farwell rotary engines. The horizontal rear elevators and the vertical rudder were controlled by two small wheels, one above the other. If you look at the propeller in the right half of the picture, you will see the two control wheels just to the left of the lower propeller blade.

The real feature of the aircraft was the use of the two Adams-Farwell rotary engines mounted horizontally on both sides of the pilot's seat. The five cylinders of each engine rotated as a single unit around a stationary crankshaft, and drove directly two tractor propellers. This is a sight that few people living today have ever seen. We are accustomed to seeing a propeller spin, but not the entire engine!

There is no mention in any published account of the plane that the engines counter-rotated to balance each other. No flywheel was necessary because the spinning cylinders acted as a giant flywheel themselves. The cooling effect of the rotating cylinders eliminated the need for water cooling with its bulky radiator. In fact, cooling was so efficient that there were no cooling fins on the cylinder heads. The net effect of the engine

design was to produce a very lightweight engine relative to the horsepower produced. Actually the engines were a redesign for aircraft installation of the rotary engine used in the Adams-Farwell automobile which had been in production since 1904.

Attending all this technical description, it would be good to report that a new era of smooth aero power was born, but in fact when the Andrews' aircraft took off from Daytona Beach in June 1910, it only flew 100 feet at a height of six feet. At that point the rear elevators vibrated loose and the machine dropped to the sand, almost totally wrecked. The pilot was unhurt, and an Andrews' spokesman was quoted as blaming the engines! Whatever the cause, no more flights were attempted, and we have found no record indicating that Andrews ever continued with the twin-engine concept. Too bad, because it would have been interesting to learn what it was like to fly an aircraft while seated between two rotary engines producing the effect of two giant gyroscopes. Would the engines have held the airplane on course and resisted a pilot's attempt to maneuver?

Several months later on September 27, a Frenchman named Roger Sommers made a successful flight in his twin-engined biplane. Like Andrews, he used two rotary engines, but in typical Gallic fashion his installation was a more logical solution. He placed one engine in front of the cockpit, and the other aft. The pulling-pushing solution had the two rotary engines spinning in opposite directions, cancelling out all torque.

Detail of the twin control wheels

Here is Edward F. Andrews, this time clinging to a glider and looking as if some giant hawk had swooped down and snatched him off the sand!

Andrews was back on the beach for further flight experiments in March 1911, but this time with a glider. One thinks of flight experimentation as progressing from a glider to an engine-powered airplane, but here is Andrews reversing the process, probably because he seemed interested mainly in flight theory. The result of his experimentation was described by him in an account published in *Aeronautics* magazine for May 1911:

"I have also been making some experiments at Daytona Beach, Florida, with a Montgomery glider. The picture shows the glider in the course of a two-mile flight which was accomplished by towing the machine behind an automobile. When the tow rope was slackened during the flight, the machine would begin to glide at a very flat angle. With this fact in view, I had intended to tow the machine into the air, then release the tow rope and glide to the earth, but owing to an accident in which the machine was smashed and my foot hurt, I did not get an opportunity to try this out.

"In closing I wish to warn other experimenters to profit by my experience and avoid all forms of towing flight. I have found this to be dangerous. A machine, which if free would be perfectly safe, is made as erratic as a child's kite by the attachment of a rope. I, for one, shall seek other means of getting into the air."

Up until 1910 only Bates and Andrews appear to have made ascensions from the beach in a powered airplane. But their efforts were really nothing more than powered hops. The beach had yet to see a *sustained* powered flight lasting more than a few seconds — not surprising when you consider that there were very few aircraft capable of sustained flight in the entire country. In fact, there were only 26 pilots licensed by the Aero Club of America, although a number of good aviators had not bothered to get a license, as there was no legal requirement to do so. Still, very few people could pilot an airplane.

Both the Wright Brothers and Glenn Curtiss were manufacturing airplanes, but to help sell their product they also taught pupils how to fly and hired a stable of pilots to fly their planes in exhibitions around the country. After all, hardly anyone had ever *seen* an airplane, much less watched one fly.

Civic leaders and hotelmen in Daytona recognized all this and decided that a flying exhibition would be the perfect tourist attraction. In February 1911 they signed a contract with Glenn Curtiss for $3,500 stipulating that one of his pilots, John A.D. McCurdy, would make a series of three flights off the beach.

John A.D. McCurdy stands in front of the Curtiss airplane. He was the fifth man in the United States and the second Canadian (the first being F.W. Baldwin) to fly a motor-driven airplane. Note the stiff collar and tie, business suit and white shoes! The glamorous flying helmets, scarfs, leather jackets and jodhpurs came later!

McCurdy, as it turned out, was his own best advance man publicizing the event. Just prior to his arrival in Daytona, Cuba had offered an $8,000 prize for the first airplane to fly from the United States to Cuba. This was a real challenge because the only previous over-water flight had been Louis Bleriot's successful flight of 23 miles across the English Channel on July 25, 1909, a flight during which he was never out of sight of land.

McCurdy decided to attempt the flight. This would be the first recorded flight of an airplane out of sight of land. McCurdy's only navigational aids were a one-dollar Ingersoll watch and a thirty-five cent compass; so he prudently sought the cooperation of the United States Navy based at Key West. As a result, four United States Navy torpedo boats were stationed along his route.

On January 30, 1911, he took off from Key West. As he approached the coast of Cuba, a leaking oil tank caused the engine to seize and McCurdy was forced to ditch in the ocean. The *U.S.S. Terry* immediately took McCurdy and his plane aboard and delivered him to the dock at Havana where the Cubans greeted him enthusiastically. Even though he fell short of his goal, he had set two new records — the longest flight ever, and the world's longest flight over water, a distance of about 90 miles.

The publicity from this flight, coming as it did just before McCurdy's visit to Daytona, greatly increased interest in his flying exhibition. However, McCurdy did not fly his airplane to Daytona.

As demonstrated by the Cuban flight, early aircraft engines were unreliable; so McCurdy's airplane arrived in Daytona by rail. The subsequent towing of the airplane from the railroad depot to the Clarendon Hotel turned into a tourist event all by itself. Crowds lined the street to gawk at the strange contraption!

This view of McCurdy's Curtiss airplane gives a good idea of the bulkiness of water-cooled engines. The flat frontal area of the big radiator does nothing for the airplane's speed!

Photo Courtesy Halifax Historical Society

History doesn't record if this was McCurdy's first flight on Daytona Beach, but it was one of the several he made during his exhibitions beginning March 28, 1911. On all his flights he carried a mechanic, one of whom can be seen sitting on the wing behind McCurdy, and to his left. As evidenced by the crowd, McCurdy's visit was a great success. On one of his flights he turned away from the safety of the beach landing strip and flew west over the Halifax River and south along Beach Street. Business came to a complete halt as clerks and customers alike emptied the shops and ran into the streets.

Photo Courtesy Dorothy Miller

Pilot Phillips Ward Page, with two helpers at the props, is about to give a pretty debutante a ride on Daytona Beach. Believe it or not, neither one of them is strapped in. Such precautions were not practiced in the very early days of flying. One just held on tight, as we see here. Page firmly grips the controls, and the lady holds on to a wing strut. The only strap in sight clinches the lady's long skirt!

McCurdy's flights made a lasting impression on the proprietors of the beachside Clarendon Hotel (now called the Howard Johnson Hotel). They contracted with W. Starling Burgess, the yacht designer turned airplane builder, to furnish an airplane and pilot to fly hotel guests during the 1912 winter season from January to April.

Burgess constructed a hangar on the beach just south of the Clarendon and sent Phillips Ward Page of Brookline, Massachusetts, to pilot his Burgess-Wright airplane. Basically it was a Wright Brothers' airplane constructed by Burgess under license with some modifications.

Phil Page was a Harvard graduate, a former newspaperman, a good tennis player and dancer — just the man to appeal to the upscale clientele of the Clarendon.

Incidentally, referring to the photograph on the opposite page, the strap around the young lady's skirt was a requisite for lady passengers in those days.

Three years earlier, when the Wright Brothers first demonstrated their successful airplanes in Europe, they took their sister Katherine along. The Wright flights took Europe by storm, and even Katherine became an instant celebrity.

Pictures of her taking her first airplane ride, with her skirt securely held in place by a string, appeared in all the newspapers. This started the highly impractical "hobble skirt" fashion!

On the right is the direct descendant of Katherine Wright's tied down skirt, the hobble skirt fashion. This example (1911) is a French version, with a large wrap-around sash and bow duplicating the string around Katherine's skirt. As you can imagine, it made walking difficult and inspired much ridicule, leading to the derisive name "Hobble." Sometimes, in its extreme form, a deep slit at the side was an absolute necessity for walking!

Photo Courtesy Rochester Central Library

BURGESS AEROPLANE

Photo Courtesy Halifax Historical Society

Early aircraft were not swift. Here we see Page and a paying passenger taking off in front of the Clarendon Hotel at Seabreeze, Florida. They are without the protection of goggles, and their airspeed is probably not more than 25 or 30 miles per hour. The passenger even retains his full brimmed hat!

Beach flying had its disadvantages. If you look at the photograph above, you will note the cross wind as indicated by the flags atop the hotel. Unless the wind was blowing up or down the beach (from the southeast or northwest) the pilot had to contend with cross winds. This often meant long waits for the wind to die down. The flags in this photograph indicate the wind was probably little more than a zephyr at ground level.

The mention of the Clarendon Hotel as being located in Seabreeze comes from the fact that for most of the first quarter of the 20th century, the Daytona area was really three cities. On the beach front was Daytona Beach, with the town of Seabreeze abutting it on the north. To the west of these two towns just across the Halifax River was Daytona. They were often referred to as the Triple Cities. On August 4, 1925, the residents of the area voted to unite, and the combined cities chose the name Daytona Beach.

Just how ideal the beach was as a takeoff and landing surface can be seen by the presence of bicycles in this photo. The tread on their wheels was half the width of the wheels on Page's airplane, yet bicycling was very popular on the hard sand before the onslaught of automobiles. Note the hangar in the background built especially for Page.

Photo Courtesy Dorothy Miller

The photograph on this page illustrates the first appearance of an airplane hangar on Daytona Beach. If we define an airport as a takeoff and landing field with provisions for aircraft shelter and service, you are looking at Florida's first airport!

The Curtiss Field at Miami Beach had previously been accorded this honor, but in fact it was almost a dead heat between the two locations. W. Starling Burgess came down to Florida and began the use of the Seabreeze location by giving his airplane five test flights on January 25, 1912, before turning the airplane over to Phillips Page.

Earlier in that same month Charles C. Witmer, the chief instructor at the Curtiss Flying School, for which the Miami Field was established, brought several landplanes and a hydroplane to Miami Beach. But all of his initial flights before the

Burgess flights were made in his hydroplane operating from the inland waterways, with student flight training from the Curtiss Field beginning shortly after the Burgess flights. Contemporary Miami newspapers made no mention of a hangar, but a later account of the Curtiss school by an eyewitness mentioned that classes were held in a tent.

In retrospect, it's not hard to understand why Daytona Beach (Seabreeze) was overlooked. It's difficult to accept the fact that a beach can be an airport! Both airfields can lay claim to being among the first 50 established airports in the United States.

The beach at Daytona continued to be used by airplanes up until about 1940, and at least seven aircraft hangars were constructed on the beach from 1912 to 1929.

This photograph, taken from the passenger side while aloft with Phillips Page, shows the Clarendon Hotel and Page's hangar just to the south. With the engine behind instead of in front, and with no enclosing fuselage, the sensation of flying in those days must have been acute!

Photo Courtesy Dorothy Miller

Phillips Page's visit in the winter of 1912 left us a small legacy. Sometime in January or February of that year at least five aerial photographs of the Ormond-Daytona area were taken from his aircraft. Four of them are shown on pages 18-21, the earliest Florida photographs known to be in existence taken from an airplane!

Perhaps the only competition for this claim is a picture taken by passenger Hayden Crosby while flying from Palm Beach in a hydroplane piloted by Walter Brookins. Crosby took at least one photograph of the Hotel Royal Poinciana in January 1912, and it was reproduced in the February 10 issue of *Aero* magazine.

Page might have taken these photos himself, attaching the camera to the vertical strut near his right shoulder. But since his twin-stick controls required the use of both hands, it's more likely that a passenger took the pictures — probably local photographer Richard LeSesne. At least one of these aerial photographs was published as a post card with LeSesne's imprint on the back.

Four miles north of the Clarendon Hotel, Page flies over Ormond Beach.

Photo Courtesy Dorothy Miller

Continuing the flight northward for a few miles to Ormond, we come to the Bretton Inn, seen here at the bottom of the picture facing on the beach. The site is now occupied by the Granada Inn.

Just to the north of the Bretton Inn, the tree-lined white stripe across the center of this view is Granada Avenue. Stretching northward from Granada is the nine-hole Ormond Golf Course, then a treeless green sward whose main hazard must have been the wind, as sand traps seem to be very scarce. Modern day golfers who think their local course is monotonous can take heart from this scene!

Note that along the back of the beach there is no Route A1A, just a small path cut through the scrub northward to an isolated beach house. Present day victims of Granada Avenue traffic jams will find this pastoral photograph hard to believe! The Halifax River can be seen in the upper-left corner.

**Approaching from the
north, this is another view
of the Clarendon Hotel.**

Photo Courtesy Dorothy Miller

Three years earlier on Valentine's Day, February 14, 1909, the old wooden Clarendon Hotel burned to the ground. This photograph shows the new Clarendon at the beginning of its second season. In those days such winter hotels were open usually from January through April, whereupon the entire staff would migrate north, often intact, to run a summer hotel in the Adirondacks or on Long Island or in the New Hampshire mountains.

As Florida hotels go, the Clarendon Hotel and the Hotel Continental on Atlantic Beach in Jacksonville were unique, being the only major Florida East Coast hotels facing on a magnificent beach. By comparison, the Ponce de Leon and the Alcazar were situated in the middle of St. Augustine; the Hotel Ormond faced west on the Halifax River; the Rockledge Hotel faced east on the Indian River, and the Royal Poinciana in Palm Beach faced west on Lake Worth and backed onto the Atlantic Ocean. The Breakers in Palm Beach faced on the ocean, but its beach could not compare with Ormond-Daytona.

In all these aerial photographs Page is not just flying low on purpose, as his engine only puts out 40 hp. Early aircraft engines were not powerful, being mostly in the range of 25 to 60 hp, and an altitude of 2,000 feet was quite high. In fact, if an airport was located in an area of high altitude, such as a mountainous region, takeoff could be difficult in the thinner air. One of the attractions of a beach airport was its very low altitude, only inches above sea level.

After the 1912 season Phillips Page never returned to Daytona and eventually went into the automobile tire business. When the United States entered World War I in 1917, he became a Navy pilot and was killed in an seaplane accident on December 17, 1917, while stationed in England.

This closer view of the Clarendon shows the intersection of what is now North Atlantic Boulevard. Modern day residents can only sigh at the sight of all those vacant oceanfront lots!

Photo Courtesy Dorothy Miller

Photo Courtesy Dorothy Miller

Somehow this picture of Page cruising just above the surf suggests that an old Burgess-Wright airplane stationed on the beach today, perhaps with a modern engine, would *still* be a popular ride!

Photo Courtesy Halifax Historical Society

Pilot Ruth Law poses with Daytona resident Colonel Charles M. Bingham just before their first flight on January 12, 1913.

By 1913 the idea of a resident pilot to offer airplane flights had become a fixture at the Clarendon Hotel. It was an ideal activity for a pilot — a way to avoid the cold northern winters while keeping flying skills sharp, and several fliers vied for the position. In 1913 the job was won by Charles Oliver, but not for himself. He was the agent for his wife, the famous pioneer woman pilot, Ruth Bancroft Law.

Ruth Law was only the fifth woman pilot to be licensed and one of about three still active in 1913. Over 5,000 people flocked to Daytona Beach on a Sunday afternoon, January 12, 1913, to see her first flight. She took Colonel C.M. Bingham as passenger on the flight that made her the first woman to pilot an airplane in Florida. Later on she became the first woman to loop an airplane, and the first woman to fly at night in Florida. And if that's not enough "firsts," her brother F. Rodman Law was a pioneer stuntman in the movies and the first person to parachute from the Statue of Liberty! Oddly enough, they were from a conservative New England family, and Ruth was graduated from an exclusive finishing school. Her mother, contemplating her unorthodox offspring, once remarked that she felt like a hen who had hatched two ducks!

Brother and sister differed in one respect, however. While Rodman was one of the first exhibition parachute jumpers, Ruth would never wear a parachute while flying. Years later when asked about this, she said, "It would have been considered cowardice."

Photo Courtesy John P. Ingle, Jr.

The lady passenger on the left is Mrs. Robert Goelet, prominent New York socialite. She took a flight with Ruth Law in February 1914 during Ruth Law's second season on the beach. Incidentally, Ruth designed all her own flying outfits, which accounts for her "different" look here. Notice her French cavalier boots.

Miss Law's aircraft was a Wright Model B with a 40-hp engine. This plane became airborne around 25–30 mph and cruised at around 35 mph. The slow speed of these early aircraft was one of the main reasons why the very early fliers were able to survive so many crashes, Charles Hamilton being the most obvious example!

Control systems were not standardized in the pioneer days, and different aircraft manufacturers featured different sys-tems. The Wright method is shown here, with two vertical control levers controlling the three basic movements of an aircraft.

The stick in Ruth's right hand is moved forward and backward to control the elevator (pitch). On the top of this lever is a shorter lever about 6 or 8 inches long. When this lever is moved to the right or left, it controls the rudder (yaw). The left hand lever is moved left or right to control the wing warp (roll).

Photo Courtesy Halifax Historical Society

Photographer: Richard H. LeSesne

Ruth Law poses in her customized Curtiss Model E pusher during the winter season of 1915.

Ruth Law flew four seasons on the beach, from 1913 through 1916. By 1915 she had developed into an able stunt pilot. In that year she and her husband visited the Curtiss Company at Hammondsport, New York, and ordered the customized Model E pusher that you see here. It featured a tricycle landing gear, a Curtiss 0X 100-hp engine, and generally beefed-up construction. The 100-hp engine was quite a step-up in power from her Wright airplane with a 40-hp engine, and made the Curtiss a kind of hot rod of that era.

The Curtiss Model E featured a control wheel which the pilot grasped with both hands, but Miss Law had learned to fly with the two-stick Wright system previously described. Consequently she had the Wright system installed on her Curtiss.

On December 17, 1915, while flying her Curtiss from the beach at Seabreeze, she became the first woman in the world to loop an airplane. Such exploits did not hurt Miss Law's reputation as a safe pilot. She could do her own engine repair, carve and replace damaged wing struts, and rig the aircraft. She always meticulously checked the entire airplane before every flight.

According to a local newspaper, Miss Law maintained two aircraft on the beach during the 1916 winter season, her Wright aircraft for passenger flights, and her Curtiss for exhibition flying. For both the 1915 and 1916 seasons she flew from two hangars in front of the Nautilus Casino just north of the Clarendon Hotel.

Ruth Law's visits at Daytona generated at least one story that still pops up in print. It goes like this: The Brooklyn Superbas (later called the Brooklyn Dodgers) had come down to Daytona Beach for spring training, and to herald their arrival someone had come up with a novel idea. Instead of having some dignitary throw the first ball from a seat in the grandstands, Ruth Law was asked to fly over the field and throw the first ball from her airplane. Wilbert Robinson, famous Dodger manager of that day and a self-styled expert at snaring high pop flies, was to be the catcher. Just before taking off, Ruth realized that no one had given her a baseball to throw. Hurriedly, one of the mechanics handed her an approximate substitute, a grapefruit! A nice juicy grapefruit is the equivalent of a cannonball if dropped from a good height, but Ruth was unaware of the physics involved. She took off from the beach and in a few minutes came over the baseball field right on line toward Robinson. At the appropriate moment she flung the grapefruit. The heavy missile arched downward, tore through Robinson's outstretched catcher's mitt, thudded on his chest, and knocked him flat on his back! Miss Law was understandably concerned over the effect of her aim, but the crowd loved it completely!

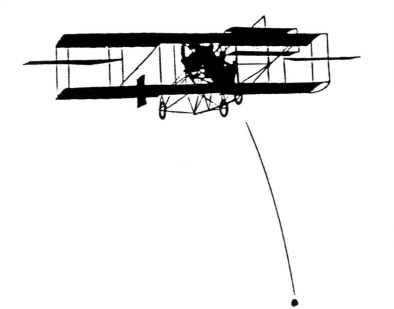

Well, it's a terrific story, but not quite the way G. Floyd Herrick remembered it. Floyd, oldest surviving member of a pioneer Daytona family, was 87 years old at the time of an interview with him on February 23, 1989, but he still recalled the grapefruit saga very clearly.

The year was 1915 and Floyd was a 13-year-old spectator at that big opening day when Ruth Law's airplane appeared overhead. The first thing Floyd recalled was that Miss Law had a passenger. It was the passenger who committed the foul deed — as a joke. They came over the field several hundred feet high, and when the passenger dropped a round object, everyone could see immediately that it was some kind of fruit. It came down, bright in the sun, straight toward Robinson. Unfortunately for our story, an ocean breeze caught it and pushed it to one side where it splattered harmlessly on the ground. The joke having fizzled, Ruth Law circled the field for another run. This time the passenger dropped a real baseball; Robinson caught it, and the season had begun. The crowd had a chuckle over the incident, and some baseball writer had the germ of an idea that ultimately developed into a timeless, reusable story!

After her Daytona years, Ruth Law tried to enlist as a pilot during World War I, but was refused. When the war was over, her husband Charles Oliver, who had managed her flying career right from the start, established the Ruth Law Flying Circus, and for several years Ruth was a highly paid barnstormer, traveling the country with a three-plane act that also included two male pilots.

Her husband was a great flying enthusiast but did not fly himself because of a nervous temperment. He worried incessantly about Ruth's flying, and this ultimately caused him to have a nervous breakdown. In consideration of her husband, Ruth retired from flying in 1922 and never resumed. She died in 1970 at the age of 79.

In this photograph taken shortly after George Gray's arrival at Ormond Beach, Gray is in the middle of the picture with his cap partly obscured by a greeter's hand. This photo represents a phenomenon of the day. Aircraft arrivals immediately drew a curious crowd!

Not long after Ruth Law arrived at the Clarendon in 1913, another pilot landed on the beach at the Clarendon. His name was George A. Gray, and he was on a cross-country flight from Jacksonville with stops at St. Augustine and Ormond. It was the first cross-country flight ever attempted in Florida, and at the finish Gray delivered to the *Daytona Daily News* the first air-mail letter to arrive in Daytona. As cross-country flights go, this must have been the safest on record, as Gray hugged the beach all the way from Jacksonville! Not to take anything from Gray, however, just a few months before, on October 1, 1912, he became the first to fly over the Adirondack Mountains (from Malone to Saranac, a distance of 85 miles) braving tricky air currents over mountains and forests where there were *no* landing fields.

Gray had intended to continue on to Palm Beach, but he changed his mind and decided to stay at Ormond, where he offered rides to guests at the Hotel Ormond and the Bretton Inn.

Gray's passenger business was very slow at first. He encountered many hotel guests who professed a fear of heights. As a result, he hit on the idea of offering very low flights. He found that passengers enjoyed flying up and down the beach, just skimming above the surf. One even came back for more flights, gradually working up to higher altitudes!

Photo Courtesy Embry-Riddle Aeronautical University

Aviator George A. Gray and his wife "Jack" Stearns Gray pose on Ormond Beach in the winter of 1915 in their Wright pusher aircraft christened *UP*.

Gray returned to Ormond two years later for the 1915 season, but his stay ended on a rather mysterious note. On March 28, 1915, about four miles north of Ormond where the beach was wild and deserted, Gray was found lying unconscious just above the water's edge. His airplane wreckage lay just offshore, partly submerged at a depth of about five feet in the surf. He had been unconscious about an hour and was badly bruised, but otherwise unhurt.

No explanation of the crash was offered in the local paper, and the same issue covering the story also carried a notice offering the aircraft wreckage for sale, as the engine was sound and the aircraft repairable. Gray immediately left the area, and his biography, *"UP,"* written years later by his wife, makes no mention of the crash.

This is a rare sight for any aviation historian — two aircraft hangars built in the first row of dunes just above the high tide mark of an ocean beach. The location was just in front of the Nautilus Casino about 200 yards north of the Clarendon Hotel. Both hangars were left over from Ruth Law's visits.

Photo Courtesy Barbara Lindley Mason

Here is the first appearance on the beach of a "tractor" airplane, the Standard H-3.

Photo Courtesy Halifax Historical Society

During the war years a company called the Standard Aero Corporation manufactured training aircraft under contract with the Army. Flight testing was ordinarily conducted near its New York plant, but rather than curtail testing in the cold winter months, they looked southward and chose the beach at Daytona as the best winter site. In January 1917 pilot Overton M. Bounds, one of the country's early fliers, brought two Standard aircraft to the beach along with multiple sets of wings and occupied the Ruth Law hangars.

All of the earliest airplanes on the beach were pushers, with the propellers behind the main wings and the pilot sitting up front exposed to the elements. The Standard Aero Corporation's airplanes were "tractor" types, with the engine and propellers in front pulling the aircraft. They were the Standard model J and model H-3 designed by Charles Healy Day, an Early Bird pilot who was a leading aircraft designer in the pioneer years.

Like most early designs, these aircraft used a water-cooled engine. The radiator had to be put somewhere; so it was perched atop the engine and attached to the top wing. Things were somewhat improved for pilot and passenger. They got to sit in an enclosed fuselage!

THE FIRST FLYING SCHOOL ON THE BEACH

Up until the end of 1916 aviation was in its pioneer era. The declaration of war by the United States against Germany on April 3, 1917, signalled the beginning of another era. Airplanes had found their first practical value — as weapons of war! Young men were anxious to become pilots in the war effort, and a need for training facilities developed. Both Phillips Ward Page and Ruth Law had given flying lessons on the beach to a few students, but no organized flying school came to Daytona Beach until America entered the war. The sequence of events leading to such a school began in Princeton, New Jersey.

A group of students at Princeton University decided to be trained as pilots in a single unit, and to this end the Princeton Flying School was begun on April 5, 1917. The first class graduated in August. Shortly thereafter this school was taken over by the West Virginia Flying Corps of Wheeling, West Virginia, which later became the West Virginia Aircraft Company.

This new company expanded the school to include civilians other than Princeton men. The beginning of winter was exceptionally cold, making training difficult; so the company decided to shift the school to Florida for the winter months. They sent their chief instructor, Frank Stanton, and one mechanic, William Lindley, also a pilot, to scout for a suitable site.

After stopovers at Jacksonville and St. Augustine, they landed at Daytona on December 31, 1917, and immediately chose the long wide beach as an ideal flight training location. An old Ruth Law hangar still stood just north of the Nautilus Casino and was available for the two Curtiss JN-4's used by the school.

Photo Courtesy Barbara Lindley Mason

Obviously it was brisk weather when the personnel of the first flying school on Daytona Beach (officially called the Daytona Flying Club) gathered to have their picture taken in January 1918 in front of a Curtiss JN-4B trainer tractor biplane.

Reading left to right, they are Edward "Ted" Parr, student from South Orange, New Jersey; Louis Senghas, student from Toronto, Canada; William "Bill" Lindley, pilot-mechanic; Frank Stanton, chief instructor; Eugene "Count" De Boliac, pilot-chief mechanic; Frank L. Boyd, student from Billings, Montana; Patrick S. Curtis, student from Billings, Montana.

Frank Stanton was already a veteran of World War I when he arrived on Daytona Beach. An Australian by birth, he served in an Australian unit attached to the British army and saw service in Africa and the invasion of the Dardanelles. From the Dardanelles he was invalided home. Eventually discharged, he emigrated in 1916 to the United States for the purpose of taking up flying. After he received his flight training, he served as an instructor at a flying school in Buffalo, New York, before joining the Princeton Flying School as an instructor. In those days and before World War I, pilot licenses were issued by a civilian aviation organization known as the Aero Club of America, and not by the Government. It wasn't until after World War I that the Government took over the issuance of pilots' licenses, at which time the numbering system began all over again. Those pilots holding Aero Club of America licenses had to reapply for the Government license.

When Frank Stanton instructed flying on the beach in 1918, he was qualified to certify pilots for the Aero Club of America pilot's license and also for the Aero Club of America Expert aviator's license.

This was William Lindley's first appearance on the beach. He fell in love with Daytona and stayed all during the twenties, becoming the most popular and well-known pilot operating from the beach. Shortly after the group picture was taken he was appointed Stanton's assistant flight instructor.

The balding, mustached "Count" De Boliac is an enigmatic figure, reputed to have flown for France earlier in the war. Whether he was a real count or not is unknown.

Fortunately, there were no significant storms during the war years or this hangar, previously used by Ruth Law, would never have survived, being just on the rear edge of the beach. Judging by the long shadows, it's early morning in the winter of 1918 and Stanton's Jenny is about to be rolled out.

Photo Courtesy Stanton Kluge

The Hangar on Beach. Seabreeze Fla.

On the left Bill Lindley is photographed about to take a break from teaching to give a celebrity a ride. On February 2, 1918, his passenger in the back seat was the comely Miss Clara Fowler of Vitagraph Film Company in New York, who was spending the winter in Daytona.

The pilots of the flying school supplemented their income by offering rides to passengers all during the 1918 winter season. With no competition, business was brisk.

We are blasé about flying today, but in those earlier times there was an aura of romance and excitement about it. An airplane was like a magnet, and the pilot seemed possessed of some arcane skill. It was common for the local Daytona papers to carry accounts of people's reactions after taking a passenger flight off the beach, and the gossip columns would often mention the names of people who took rides.

We don't know who this old gent is, but he was obviously a passenger with Bill Lindley sometime around 1918. During the winter season the weather could be warm at beach level and decidedly cool several thousand feet up in the air. Lindley kept extra jackets, helmets and goggles to ensure the comfort of his passengers.

Photos Courtesy Barbara Lindley Mason

Photo Courtesy Barbara Lindley Mason

This photograph gives a good idea of how the beach was an endless runway! The Nautilus Casino, which was destroyed by fire in February 1921, can be seen just below the wings and to the left of the landing gear. Note the two airplane hangars just to the left of the Casino on the bottom edge of the picture. The date of this photo is between January and April 1918.

The endless stretch of beach must have instantly appealed to someone like Frank Stanton, chief instructor of the Daytona Flying Club. When it came time to entrust one of his precious Jennies to a soloing student, he could simply instruct the student to fly up the beach for ten or fifteen miles and then fly back the same way — never leaving the airport! And when the student landed, Stanton would never have to worry that the student would undershoot or overshoot the runway!

It would be fine to say that the school finished its first season without incident, but it was not to be. On April 1, 1918, Bill Lindley took off from the beach with a student, Keith Henry, but the aircraft lost power, nosed down, and crashed on Butler Boulevard at the corner of Grandview Avenue. Fortunately Keith Henry only suffered a few scratches and Lindley was confined to a hospital for a brief period with a wrenched back. News of the crash spread like wild fire, and a huge crowd collected from miles around. Inevitably, parts of the airplane became souvenirs, but it didn't matter because the airplane was a total loss. A much greater blow to the school occurred two days later on April 3 when the Government closed all civilian-run flying schools for the duration of the war. Flying on the beach came to an abrupt halt — but not for long. The real aerial invasion was about to begin!

The Butler Boulevard bust! This view, with engine awry, was taken by Richard LeSesne, whose Daytona photographic career began almost exactly with Charles Hamilton's appearance at Ormond.

Photo Courtesy Halifax Historical Society

Photographer: Richard H. LeSesne

THE CARLSTROM FIELD INVASION

Hold onto your hats! Here comes the Keystone Kops of the airways — the Carlstrom Field Army pilots! That may sound like blasphemy, but old Daytona newspapers bear us out. But first, a little background.

During the American involvement in World War I, the Army established Carlstrom Field, just outside of Arcadia, Florida, as one of its main pilot training facilities. The field was about 150 miles southwest of Daytona as the crow flies, and from 1918 to 1924 (when the field was closed), a constant stream of Carlstrom aircraft landed on Daytona Beach.

The beach was on a major route for cross-country flight training, and thus was a tempting stopover for glamorous Army pilots. The beach was also a major weekend destination, with Army pilots putting up at beachside hotels and joining in the local revelries.

For example, on Saturday, February 15, 1919, a flight of eight Curtiss training planes from Carlstrom landed on the beach. They had flown over for the sole purpose of watching race car driver Ralph De Palma try for a speed record. Naturally, once arrived, they stayed for the weekend!

From today's viewpoint the use of Government airplanes and fuel for private pleasure would be a scandal, but the local papers of the day reported it routinely, and it never seemed to be curbed. Even so, the real cost to the taxpaper was the unending series of mishaps that the Army pilots experienced while landing and taking off from the beach. It was an uninterrupted chorus of busted props, bent landing gears, and buckled wings!

This Carlstrom Field pilot and his Le Pere Fighter tried to take off in June 1919 from Daytona Beach. As the aircraft picked up speed, a small boy darted across the beach. The unlucky pilot had to swerve into the surf with the results shown on the right. Note the splintered propeller.

Photo Courtesy Halifax Historical Society

Here is what W.C. Green saw when he looked up just after his narrow escape! Local photographer Clark G. Smith took this photograph of the wreck described below and made a post card of it.

Photo Courtesy Halifax Historical Society
Photographer: Clark G. Smith

Mack Senneth would have loved this one. It seems that a flying circus of five airplanes stopped at Daytona Beach on their way from Carlstrom Field to Jacksonville, Florida, where they were scheduled to perform stunt flying. They landed at Daytona Beach on the afternoon of June 24, 1919.

When they were ready to leave, the high tide at that hour afforded only a small strip of hard sand on which to run. Undeterred, Curtiss bomber #44790 started north up the beach and rapidly gained speed. Unfortunately, the pilot must have lost his concentration, because he drifted to the left. The right wheel continued to run on the hard sand, but the left wheel dug into the soft sand of the upper beach. This threw the aircraft left, to the west, and before the pilot could stop it, the plane pranced up the face of the first dune.

W.C. Green stood on this very same dune and saw the plane headed his way. Either because of quick reflexes or a weakness of knees, Green keeled over backward and slid down the back of the dune just as the huge churning propeller pulled the plane over the crest at the identical spot where he had stood a moment before. He arose unscathed and looked back to see the plane perched on its nose with its tail almost perpendicular, just as you see in the above photograph.

Fortunately, the pilot Lt. E.W. Mauselmann and mechanic David Davis were unhurt, and spectator W.C. Green had a lifetime memory to recount to his grandchildren!

Here's another view of the same wreck that menaced W.C. Green.

Photo Courtesy Barbara Lindley Mason
Photographer: Clark G. Smith

Another nose-down job! When they weren't hitting cars, upending in soft sand, or landing in the surf due to fog, they might run into flotsam and jetsam! On May 17, 1919, the Carlstrom flier in this photo landed safely and then tripped on a palmetto log!

Photo Courtesy Halifax Historical Society

Was pilot Young lucky or unlucky? Read his story and decide for yourself. On March 12, 1922, Mr. Young was a visitor to Daytona Beach, having just parked his rotary powered Sopwith biplane safely on the upper sands of the beach north of the Clarendon Hotel. Just down the beach three Army fliers were preparing to take off for their return trip to Carlstrom Field. Lt. R.C. McDonald was the pilot; the other two officers in the front cockpit were his passengers. Desiring to help, pilot Young moved out on the beach and acted as traffic cop, holding back automobiles until the departing aircraft could become airborne. With the way now cleared, the Army plane started its takeoff run up the beach. On it came northward toward pilot Young, faster and faster, until it had almost attained flying speed. At that point the rudder jammed.

Photo Courtesy Halifax Historical Society

Photographer: Charles Grenell

The above photograph was taken shortly after the crash. The innocent bystanding Sopwith is on the right. Note the rotary engine with propeller sheared off. A gaping hole can be seen in the fuselage just to the left of the man who is grasping a bracing wire. The ferocity of the slide can be gauged by the sand piled up on the lower fuselage of the Army plane.

With Lt. McDonald helpless to prevent it, the plane spun left, where its great forward speed put it into a vicious sideways slide. The slide tore the wheels from their rims and jackknifed the landing gear, dropping the fuselage to the ground where the slide continued with the lower wings acting like a giant single ski.

Pilot Young could only stare in total helplessness as the sliding aircraft slammed into his Sopwith. The upper wing of the errant craft, now at a lower level because of the collapsed landing gear, sliced through the Sopwith's gas tank and impaled the fuselage straight through the cockpit. The collision tore off the Sopwith's propeller, broke the landing gear, splintered the wings, and instantly grounded pilot Young! Fortunately, the three Army fliers suffered only relatively minor injuries, but the Carlstrom Field reputation for calamities remained intact!

Another view of the same wreck, with the Sopwith on the left. Wrecks make great tourist attractions!

In all fairness to the Carlstrom fliers, they were not the only ones to have adventures on the beach. Here is a civilian accident, date and pilot unknown. The aircraft is obviously a Curtiss JN-4D, the famed "Jenny." This photograph seems to be an archetype of all crashes, or perhaps the way a crash would look if depicted by a cubist painter!

Photo Courtesy Halifax Historical Society

The frequency of crashes, especially as related to the Jenny, could often be traced to its Curtiss OX-5 engine. In its original version, believe it or not, the engine was designed for a life expectancy of only 50 hours! There was a solid reason for this. When the United States government started a rapid build-up to train pilots in 1917 for World War I, there was a sudden demand for mechanics and skilled aircraft factory workers that was impossible to adequately fill in a short time. So the decision was made to produce a simple aircraft engine of short life that would be replaced rather than rebuilt. This eliminated the need for large repair depots staffed by skilled aircraft technicians who simply didn't exist!

The OX-5 engine itself had a rugged block and well built crankshaft, pistons, and piston rods, but the valve system, ignition, and cooling system were the weak links. Although simple to manufacture and install, they were the components that dictated the 50-hour life. When ex-Army fliers bought cheap surplus Jennies after World War I and went barnstorming, they often had to become mechanics and plumbers in self-defense!

All during the 1920's pilots and mechanics tinkered with the OX-5 engine to improve performance. A revamping of the valve system, the purchase of an expensive Swiss magneto or a change to dual ignition, and eventually even the conversion of the cooling system from water-cooling to air-cooling finally produced an engine that was still being widely used well into the 1940's.

But oh, those early teething problems! In the 1920's there were plenty of instances where OX-5's used on the beach would experience power loss at awkward moments. In this book Bill Lindley experienced three such power failures just on takeoff alone.

A typical group of Carlstrom airplanes (Le Pere Fighters and Curtiss JN-4D's) draws the inevitable crowd while parked just south of the Main Street pier.

Photo Courtesy Halifax Historical Society

In spite of all the mishaps, Carlstrom fliers still kept coming to the beach! It must have been the immediate postwar euphoria! During 1919 a local paper reported almost daily arrivals of the Carlstrom pilots as they stopped enroute to Jacksonville on cross-country flights.

They also landed on the beach to recruit young men for the flying service and sometimes put on air shows. As many as nine Army airplanes would be parked on the beach during a weekend. Naturally they were a great tourist attraction, and local merchants welcomed them with open arms. A commanding officer at Carlstrom Field wrote to the local Chamber of Commerce with the following complaint: "Fliers (from Carlstrom) often tell me that the greatest trouble in landing is to avoid automobiles which appear unexpectedly just as the planes are settling onto the beach and usually stop right in the path of the plane."

Anxious to please, the local fathers were quick to mark off a landing area for the visitors. They even personally directed traffic in one instance, holding automobiles and pedestrians in check while the airplanes took off and landed. It was not an exact science, however. At least one automobile slipped through the cordon and promptly struck an airplane!

Another example of the casualness of the era can be seen in this photograph of a Carlstrom Le Pere Fighter parked on the beach, bedecked in a colorful wartime camouflage of green, blue and white. Youngsters could touch the airplanes or huddle in the shade of a wing without being shooed away — the pilots were probably too busy swimming in the surf!

Photo Courtesy Halifax Historical Society
Photographer: Charles Grenell

Another type of Carlstrom aircraft to visit the beach was this De Haviland 4 bomber seen on the right. Such open air parking raises a question. Did the salt air damage airplanes? The authors sought out old-time pilots who might answer such questions, but the only one still living who flew off the beach at Daytona seems to be pioneer pilot Glenn Messer of Birmingham, Alabama. Messer remembered that preventive maintenance was very simple. As seen here, beach pilots covered their engines and cockpits with a tarpaulin. Periodically they would also wipe off the salt from the engines with a damp rag.

Photo Courtesy Halifax Historical Society

WRECKED BY FALLING MARCH 16th 1919

Despite the numerous Carlstrom crashes, only one military pilot was killed on the beach. It was an especially sad affair and received national publicity because it involved an outstanding war hero. Major David McKelvey Peterson of Honesdale, Pennsylvania, (seen on the left) visited Daytona Beach in March 1919 on a trip from Carlstrom Field. While taking off from the beach on March 16, his airplane suddenly nosed down and crashed from a height of about 75 feet. Peterson was killed instantly, and his passenger Lt. F.X. Paversick was seriously injured.

Photo Courtesy Barbara Lindley Mason

Here is Peterson's aircraft shortly after the crash. Major Peterson was an ace in World War I, credited with five official kills while flying with an American squadron. He had originally gone to France as an ambulance driver, but later transferred to the famed Lafayette Escadrille, with whom he flew until America entered the war. Oddly enough, although he is credited with 18 unofficial kills in the Lafayette Escadrille, none of these became official, and his five official kills were compiled in his later service with an American squadron. Quentin Roosevelt, son of Teddy Roosevelt, was shot down and killed while a member of the squadron commanded by Peterson.

Photo Courtesy Barbara Lindley Mason

THE BARNSTORMERS

Here's Ervin Ballough taxiing his "Canuck" on the beach sometime during the 1919-1920 winter season. Actually he is in the leading edge of the surf, and you can see a little rooster tail of water behind his tail skid. All during the tourist season, while offering airplane rides, the tail of his plane carried the macabre lettering, "We furnish the..." with a wreath painted just below the lettering! This might be part of the reason why he only stayed one season!

Photo Courtesy Halifax Historical Society

Shortly after World War I was over, the Government began to sell off their surplus aircraft, principally the Curtiss JN-4D trainer. Ex-Army pilots anxious to continue flying could buy these Jennies for as little as $500. Remember, there were no airlines. Therefore, the main sources of income for pilots were to be an instructor, offer rides, and put on air shows. With few permanent airports, pilots became gypsies, operating out of cow pastures and fairgrounds all over the country. The barnstorming era had begun!

The first of this new breed to arrive at the beach with a surplus Jenny was Daytona's own outstanding contribution to aviation, Ervin Edward Ballough. "Ervie," as he was called locally, was born and raised in a pioneer Daytona family and took his first airplane ride in 1914 with Ruth Law. From that moment on he was determined to be a pilot. After starting out as an aviation mechanic, he learned to fly in the Canadian Air Force in 1917, and proved to be such a talented pilot that he was kept as an instructor.

After the war he hit the front pages when he landed a Jenny on the roof of an Army Quartermaster warehouse at Newark, New Jersey, and then took off — the first time a pilot had performed such a feat. It was well documented because he had a photographer aboard!

He was also the first pilot to provide on-the-spot news reporting by radio from an airplane, and the first to perform power line patrols. None of the above flying activities adequately conveys his superb flying skill, but the following true story certainly gives a hint.

During the 1920's Ballough once worked for Bill Kidder at the Curtiss Northwest Airport just north of Minneapolis-St. Paul, and one day Ballough tested a new Curtiss airplane. Just as he was putting the airplane into a loop, the control stick came out! To appreciate what happened next, look at the photograph below and notice how the control cables emerge from the fuselage. Just to the left of the letter "B" in BAL, two cables emerge from black circles and extend to the tail, where they control the vertical rudder and the horizontal elevators. Just to the left of the letter "D" in DAYTONA, a single cable emerges to control the ailerons at the end of the lower wings.

Returning to our story, when the control stick came out, Ballough climbed out of the cockpit and flew the airplane by pulling the various control wires just described! Clinging to the side of the fuselage while occasionally reaching into the cockpit to control the throttle, he nursed the airplane to an almost normal landing in a field near the airport. It would have been completely normal, except that a gust of wind blew the plane into a telephone pole. As it was, Ballough walked away with nothing but a black eye!

After his arrival on the beach with his new Canuck in 1919, Ballough stayed for the entire 1919-1920 winter season, taking up passengers and stunting in local weekend air shows. Old timer Floyd Herrick of Daytona was a teenager then, and he still remembers his friendship with Ballough. Vivid in Floyd's mind is a story Ballough once told him about a local businessman named John Barbe.

John owned the beachside Barbe Hotel from where he often watched Ballough give rides to tourists. One day he came down onto the sand where Ballough was trying to drum up a little business. It was 1920 and, as you can see on the following pages, competition was stiff.

Ballough was charging ten dollars for a ride. Barbe, living up to his name, tried to barb Ballough with the following remark, "I'd take a ride with you if I thought I'd get my money's worth."

Ervin Ballough stands up in the cockpit just after he completed the first flight of a land-based airplane from New York to Daytona Beach. The date was November 13, 1919, and the passenger in the front seat for the whole trip was a New York banker named Alfred Borden. Ballough's airplane was a JN-4C ("Canuck") — a Curtiss Jenny manufactured under license in Canada.

Photo Courtesy Halifax Historical Society

Auto racing and stunt flying were often featured on the same program during weekend festivities on the beach. This photograph symbolizes the camaraderie of the two groups with Ervie Ballough riding as passenger with E.G. Yost in his *Traylor Special* sometime in the winter season of 1920.

Photo Courtesy Barbara Lindley Mason

This, as it turned out, was a tactical error. "I'll tell you what," Ervie said. "You take a ride with me, and if you think you didn't get your money's worth, I'll give back your money."

The unsuspecting Barbe accepted, was carefully strapped into the front cockpit, and in a few minutes they were aloft. Whereupon Ballough proceeded to demonstrate his entire and extensive repertoire. He started out with slow rolls and then did snap rolls. He flew right side up, upside down, and even sideways. He did loops, stalls and spins. He compressed all this into five furious flying minutes, executing all known maneuvers and perhaps several stunts not yet invented. Finally, when about to descend, Ballough looked down and noted that there were no automobiles or strollers in the immediate vicinity of the Main Street ocean pier. Conceiving a grand finale, he put the Jenny into a screaming dive.

In those days the opening under the pier that allows cars driving on the beach to pass through was wider than it is today. Ballough bottomed out of his dive several feet above the beach and thundered through the opening with several feet clearance all around. He had so much speed from his dive that he was able to pull up immediately into another loop just above the pier. His imagination now exhausted, Ballough finally landed.

As he unbuckled Barbe and helped him down from the plane, Ballough inquired if Barbe felt he had gotten his money's worth. The ashen, shaken Barbe uttered not a word. As soon as his feet were firmly planted on the sand, he shook off Ballough's helping hand. At first wobbling and stumbling, Barbe gradually regained his sense of balance, and when last seen he was in a dead run for his hotel!

During the rest of the twenties Ballough flew mostly in other parts of the country, making occasional flying visits to the beach to visit his parents and friends.

Ballough gained a national reputation in the late twenties when he flew in two coast-to-coast air races, finishing second in class A in 1927 and second in class B in 1928. In 1930 he joined Eastern Air Transport and became a million-mile captain. Always known for leading a somewhat intemperate life, he failed to pass his pilot's physical examination in 1940 and had to leave Eastern. He later flew briefly for Chalk's Flying Service before finally returning to Daytona. He died at age 54 on May 19, 1948.

This brief biography seems fitting, and not just because he was a hometown boy. Many of his fellow pilots and other knowledgeable aviation people considered him an extremely gifted and skilled pilot, worthy to be ranked on the same skill level with such legendaries as Bert Acosta, Jimmy Doolittle and Frank Clarke. In one published article, E.M. "Matty" Laird, famed airplane designer, is quoted as remarking about Ballough that, "He could fly an airplane as well as or better than anyone else."

Photo Courtesy Halifax Historical Society

The general public embraced war-time pilots in an aura of glamour and respect; therefore, it made good sense for barnstorming pilots to hold on to their rank after discharge. In the above photograph we have Captain J.O. Jorstad's airplane, *Blue Bird*, awaiting passengers in front of the Clarendon Hotel during the 1919-1920 winter season. Jorstad and his partner R.C. "Tex" Marshall arrived on the beach with their surplus Jennies on December 23, 1919.

Jorstad's *Blue Bird* (shown on the previous page) had a brief stay at Daytona Beach. Jorstad flew it down to Palm Beach, and while there his partnership with Tex Marshall was dissolved. As part of the dissolution contract, Tex Marshall took title to the *Blue Bird* and went down to Palm Beach to fly it back. While enroute north in March 1920 with a passenger, he landed on the golf course at Rockledge for gas. On takeoff he lost power and crashed into two orange trees on the course. Fortunately, nobody was hurt.

Photo Courtesy Barbara Lindley Mason

One of the many weekend auto-aerial events was a race between H.F. Alexander in his Duesenberg Special and Tex Marshall in his *Nautilus* Jenny. The race was held in February 1920, and the photographer caught the two contestants just as the flagman dropped his flag to signal the start. It was a non-event. Marshall won by four miles!

Photo Courtesy Barbara Lindley Mason

Pilots Marshall and Palmer confer in this rare snapshot of early hangars on the beach.

After Captain J.O. Jorstad departed, his place in partnership with Tex Marshall was quickly taken by Lt. Frank Palmer. The 1920 winter season was competitive, with as many as eight pilots and their Jennies offering rides on the beach. The weather was not cooperative; so the pickings must have been slim.

At the end of the season in early May, Marshall and Palmer decided to try their luck in Ohio. They intended to ship their airplanes north, but a rail freight embargo forced them to decide on a cross-country flight.

That's a simple matter today, but in 1920 there were practically no airports on that rugged route. It was decided that Marshall's wife was to go ahead by train. At some communities where they planned to land she would scout for a suitable landing area, and then mark it with a huge cross of wrapping paper bought from a local grocery store.

The whole crazy adventure over hostile hills and menacing mountains with inaccurate maps and balky engines, all the way from Seabreeze, Florida, to Findlay, Ohio, finally ended up as an intriguing chapter in the book *Barnstorming* by Martin Caidin.

Who Forgot an Airplane?

That anyone should actually be capable of forgetting an airplane may seem incredible. Yet the thing has been done, as may be seen from the story which follows—and which is authentic.

About a year ago a black JN flew into the airdrome of the Dayton-Wright Co., at Dayton, Ohio. It carried two men who inquired whether they might leave their machine on the field for a day or so, and stated that they would return for it in

A MYSTERIOUS "JENNIE"—THE AIRPLANE SOMEBODY FORGOT

that length of time. That was the last the airdrome saw of the two men. Inquiries as to who might be the owner of the bus proved without avail and nobody ever put in a claim for it. As the machine takes up valuable space, the Dayton-Wright Co. would like to hear from its owner, who should claim it without delay, else the JN will be disposed of for the payment of storage charges.

The accompanying illustration of the mysterious "Jennie" seems to show that it is of rather ancient vintage, belonging apparently to the JN-4B type. The following inscription appears on the sides of the fuselage: Marshall-Palmer Air Service, Frank Palmer, Pilot.

Photo Courtesy Embry-Riddle Aeronautical University

Shortly after Tex Marshall and Frank Palmer arrived in Ohio, they were both hired as Air Mail pilots for the U.S. Post Office Department. Naturally they no longer needed their own Jennies. This clipping from *Aviation* magazine dated June 27, 1921, illustrates how they "stored" Frank Palmer's airplane!

FLYING HUCKSTERS

In 1920 there were very few airports in Florida. In fact, there were no permanent landing fields in southern Florida at all. That made Daytona a magnet for fliers coming south, and on February 11, 1920, three more Jennies landed on the beach. They were the Wrigley Flying Circus, the first civilian circus to visit Daytona Beach. They were examples of a new wave — the airplane as a flying billboard, the pilot as a traveling promoter. Wrigley sponsored the three Jennies for a tour of the east and midwest, and when they arrived in Daytona, they delivered a shipment of Wrigley's Spearmint Chewing Gum to local warehouses — perhaps Florida's first interstate air freight.

Photo Courtesy Halifax Historical Society

The three Wrigley planes are seen here parked near the Clarendon Hotel. *Spearmint No. 1* **was flown by Elmer Partridge, a pioneer flier who had built his own plane and taught himself to fly in 1910.** *Spearmint No. 2* **was piloted by Paul "Slim" Milnor, formerly an instructor for two years in the Royal Flying Corps. E. Nimmo Black flew** *Spearmint No. 3.*

Here is a scarce bird flown by an Early Bird! The airplane is an Aeromarine A-39-B biplane with a 100-hp Curtiss OXX-6 engine and featuring its characteristic very high upper wing. The Early Bird pilot is Harry Copland, who learned to fly a Wright pusher when he was only 15. The checkered paint job on the Aeromarine carries the lettering, "THE BLADE IN THE PLAID BOX," advertising Lenox Hack Saws.

Photo Courtesy Halifax Historical Society
Photographer: Charles Grenell

The following year, 1921, brought two more flying salesmen to the beach. The first to arrive was Harry Depew Copland flying an Aeromarine biplane with a two-passenger front seat. He landed on February 6, 1921, completing the first flight ever from Maine to Florida. Percy H. Spencer, owner of the airplane, was a passenger for the entire trip, which took them nearly two months. It was a promotional tour to advertise Lenox Hack Saws manufactured by the American Saw and Manufacturing Company. Both men stayed for the winter season giving rides and performing weekend stunting exhibitions.

While flying off the beach, Copland experienced the mishap that inevitably had to happen. He was headed north above the beach, coming in for a landing. A large open Packard touring car with a chauffeur and two occupants was also headed north on the beach. (You might say that Copland was a chauffeur too, as he had two passengers in the front cockpit.) At any rate, neither chauffeur saw the other, and Copland proceeded to demonstrate that airplanes, like autos, also have blind spots.

He landed on the rear of the car. By some aberration of the law of averages, no one was really hurt at all, but the participants must have been six of the most startled people ever known! Mrs. E.L. Smith of Binghamton, New York, was in the rear of the car and sustained a few scratches, which she probably wore as trophies considering the extreme rarity of the event. Most certainly she was the life of the tea parties when she returned to Binghamton!

Incidentally the airplane suffered a broken landing gear, a shattered propeller, and a crumpled left wing tip, but was soon flying again. Imagine the rash of lawsuits if such a thing were to happen today!

Harry Copland must have been very embarrassed about the whole thing. The Air and Space Museum in Washington, D.C., has his log book covering his Florida visit. Sure enough, on the day of the accident (March 18, 1921) he dutifully recorded the damage sustained by his airplane and explained that it resulted from striking an "obstruction"!

Pilot A.M. Alcorn's Curtiss Oriole must have been a colorful sight and perhaps a magnet for the ladies who wanted to take a ride in an airplane. In harmony with its name, it was colored like the oriole, the body being orange and the wings yellow and black.

Photo Courtesy Halifax Historical Society

Photographer: Charles Grenell

The second flying promoter to arrive on the beach was A. M. Alcorn, pilot of a Curtiss Oriole owned by the Simmons Hardware Company of Philadelphia. Alcorn was hired to promote the Keen Kutter tools and cutlery, and was certainly the first hardware salesman in the world to travel exclusively by plane. He covered practically every important city on the Atlantic seaboard, and prior to his coming, hardware dealers would give every purchaser of a Keen Kutter product a numbered coupon. The dealer would keep one half of the coupon and the purchaser the other half. On the day Alcorn arrived a drawing would be held. The holder of the lucky numbers would get a free ride in Alcorn's plane. That was a big thrill in those days!

Alcorn began his flying promotion job on Armistice Day (November 11, 1918) and was still at it when he landed at Daytona Beach on February 14, 1920. Immediately he found himself reunited with an old flying buddy from Royal Flying Service days, the aforementioned Harry Copland. That same day the two flying hucksters took local photographer Charles Grenell aloft to secure pictures of their emblazoned aircraft. Grenell rode in one airplane and then the other to take photographs of the Copland and Alcorn airplanes.

Photo Courtesy Vivian Robinson

Photographer: Charles Grenell

The airplane as a billboard reached its height when Bill Lindley sold advertising space on the fuselage of his Jenny around 1922. The race car is his *Lindley Special*, powered by the same type of engine that powered his Jenny — the Curtiss OX-5.

Lindley is seated behind the wheel of his car in this photograph which epitomized his energy, ingenuity and versatility. Yet for all of his drive, he is remembered by Early Bird pilot Glenn Messer as a man of irrepressible good humor. "Jolly Bill Lindley" was often his epithet in the local newspapers. Perhaps that explains why he was so successful in selling space on his airplane! Bill's mother Amelia Bishop has an ad for her Dixie Hotel just above the lower wing. One can't help but wonder if the real moneymaker in this enterprise didn't turn out to be the man who did the lettering!

Looking like an aged oil painting, this fast deteriorating product of a beach concessionaire's art depicts Bill Lindley's Curtiss JN-4. The man in the foreground is unidentified.

Here's another ad job on a Bill Lindley Jenny, although this one is somewhat obscured by the man in the bow tie. The complete ad reads RIO VISTA ON THE HALIFAX, touting a large real estate development started during the Florida boom of the early twenties and featuring the Riviera Hotel, a golf course, boat dock, riding stables, and adjacent building lots. Alas, the project went broke with the collapse of the real estate boom in 1926.

This photograph has an interest aside from the subject matter because it was taken by a beach photographer around 1923-1924 using a camera of the type that develops on the spot. The resulting image, affixed to metal, resembles an old tintype. Such images tend to darken with time and rarely survive very long. This one, even with the crackles, is especially good. Because a beach photographer took the picture, we suspect that the man in the bow tie was a passenger wishing to have a souvenir of his flight.

A POPULAR TRIO

Frank Stanton poses (with the beach in the background) in December 1919. Note the oil drum standing in the dunes. Pumping from such drums was the main method of refueling airplanes on the beach during the teens and the twenties.

Photo Courtesy Stanton Kluge

Frank Stanton was back on the beach in December 1919, still chief instructor of the Daytona Flying Club owned by the West Virginia Aircraft Company. This time he brought three Jennies. His two assistant pilots were Bill Lindley and Gustav "Slim" Ekstrom, who was making his first appearance on the beach.

Incidentally, Stanton once had a brief stint in the movies. In the summer of 1918 while flying at Princeton, New Jersey, he played the Russian pilot (and did the flying scenes) in the silent film, *Rasputin, The Black Monk,* starring Montagu Love and Julia Dean.

Photo Courtesy Barbara Lindley Mason

In this late afternoon photograph, Frank Stanton (in white shirt) stands by the tail of his plane conversing with a man clad in the typical formal attire of the day. Even the little boy on the right and the couple sitting on a blanket next to him look like they've just returned from church! The other Jenny is flown by Bill Lindley.

Frank Stanton and Bill Lindley returned to the beach in December 1920, still working for the West Virginia Aircraft Company through a subsidiary, the Rahe Flying School. This was the last season together on the beach for Frank and Bill. In late April 1921 Frank Stanton returned to Kansas City where the Rahe School was based. Not long afterwards he left the flying business and eventually became an executive for a textile mill in South Carolina.

Lindley had just married a Daytona Beach girl, the former Jean Louise Wilder, whose brother was the nationally known novelist and screen writer Robert Wilder. Ever the beach enthusiast, Lindley decided to stay and see if he could be the first pilot to conduct a flying business the year round. This was the real beginning of Lindley's prominence and popularity as the number one flier on the beach.

Bill Lindley was popular enough to be featured in this photo post card sold at local outlets in 1921. It's his typical pose, with wide stance and arms akimbo.

Photo Courtesy Halifax Historical Society

Bill Lindley poses with his wife Jean. Some months before this picture was taken, Lindley was flying above the beach when he ran low of gas. He landed on an isolated stretch of beach just opposite the home of a prominent local dentist, Dr. William W. Wilder. Mrs. Wilder was home, and Lindley asked if he could use the telephone. Daughter Jean Louise was also home, and it was love at first sight! Bill and Jean were married on March 12, 1921. Jean was only 16!

Photo Courtesy Vivian Robinson

Born in Chicago, Illinois, in 1894, Bill Lindley first became an aircraft mechanic and then a pilot. It's not certain exactly when he first soloed, but he was a full fledged pilot by the summer of 1917, and was only prevented from serving overseas in World War I when he broke his arm while cranking an airplane motor.

By the time he decided to make Daytona his home base, he had served in the Army Air Corps as an instructor, flown throughout the midwest with the Mabel Cody Flying Circus, and served as a pilot in the Air Mail Service. Extremely likeable, good natured, and a complete extrovert, he was the ideal emissary for aviation on the beach. At first he located his flying activities around the Main Street fishing pier, but as the congestion of people and automobiles grew in the mid-twenties, he moved his operations several miles down the beach — the only instance we know of where the local airport was pushed further out by the town's growth but still retained the same runway!

The handbill on the right was distributed by Bill Lindley in the fall of 1921. He probably handed it out to tourists right on the beach. Bill "borrowed" the airplane illustration from a magazine ad put out by the Curtiss Aeroplane and Motor Corporation.

Photo Courtesy Barbara Lindley Mason

FLY

=== WITH ===

Pilot Lindley

and see the Triple Cities from the air

Safest place in the world to fly

SPECIAL RATES BY APPOINTMENT

Daytona Beach Flying School
On the Beach Near the Pier

Another pilot who based his flying operations on the beach during most of the twenties was Gustav "Slim" Ekstrom. He first came to Daytona in December 1919, when he was a co-instructor with Frank Stanton and Bill Lindley, and like Lindley he fell in love with the beach.

Gustav soloed on December 6, 1916, in Newport News, Virginia. Immediately after soloing he joined a barnstorming flying circus. In 1917 he became an instructor at the Princeton Flying School in Princeton, New Jersey, with Frank Stanton, and when Stanton located the Flying School on Daytona Beach in 1919, Ekstrom joined him again.

Contrary to appearances in the photograph on the left, Ekstrom does not have a misshapen left arm and hand. He's just reaching back over the top of the lower wing. He did have a different type of handicap, however. He stuttered. In spite of this, he became a Pan American pilot in 1928, and flew for them until his retirement in 1955. The stuttering problem was circumvented by detailing his co-pilot to handle all radio conversation.

Local photographer Reeve Hilty took this photograph of "Slim" Ekstrom standing by his Jenny around 1925.

Photo Courtesy Mrs. Gustav Ekstrom

Photographer: Reeve Hiltry

BEACH FLYING WAS CROWDED

Nowhere else in the world were people so intertwined with aviation as they were on Daytona Beach!

Photo Courtesy Barbara Lindley Mason

Here is proof positive of the crowded flying conditions on the beach in February 1920. The above photograph was taken on the Main Street pier looking north to the Clarendon Hotel on the upper left. Notice the row of oil drums dividing the distant beach just to the right of the Clarendon. The automobiles used the beach to the left of the drums; the airplanes had their landing strip on the right. Bathers, wishing to reach the ocean, must have made frantic dashes! In the foreground the taxiing airplane on the right is the *Poland Springs,* owned and piloted by Alfred Tunstall. The airplane flying just above the *Poland Springs* appears to be heading for the same opening under the pier that Ervie Ballough used!

Photo Courtesy Halifax Historical Society

Here's the airport that was located downtown! The Jenny behind the cars is within a few yards of the nearest buildings in Daytona Beach, and only 100 yards from the business section which begins at the land end of the Main Street pier from which this photograph was taken. Pilots who stayed the winter season rented cottages or apartments only a short stroll from their airplanes.

Photo Courtesy Halifax Historical Society

**Pilot Stuart Davies takes off just north of the Main Street pier
(under somewhat crowded conditions!) in the winter of 1921.**

The best way to look at this photograph is to imagine a large excavation project tearing up the road that borders your local airport. While the work is in progress, the local fathers look for a way to reroute the traffic. Noting the broad straight cement airport runway running parallel to the road, the city fathers simply reroute the auto traffic right down the busy airport runway. Now that's ridiculous, right? But that's just what you're looking at here — airplane and cars simultaneously using the same roadway...or runway...or freeway...or...well, what would you call it?

The airplane pictured here is a Jenny piloted by Stuart Davies. Like Copland's *Lenox* airplane, and Alcorn's *Keen Kutter,* Davies' airplane also did a little advertising. In bold lettering on the wings and fuselage it was announced as the *Utica* plane, calling attention to Utica, New York, as a summer resort and commercial center.

Davies came to the beach four consecutive seasons, beginning in December 1920. On first arrival he brought two mechanics, Fred Manziger and Lynn W. Walker. Walker also doubled as Davies' stuntman.

Photo Courtesy Halifax Historical Society

Photographer: William L. Coursen

Only on a wide beach at low tide could so many automobiles line up abreast at the start of a race!

What is an automobile racing photograph doing in an aviation book? It's here because it is the only known photograph of a hangar built by Bill Lindley in December 1921.

Lindley built it to serve a double purpose — as a hangar for his Jenny and a grandstand and starter point for the weekend auto races that were very popular on the beach in the early twenties. If you look closely, you can see Lindley's Jenny in front of the hangar opening.

The first car in the line-up at the right of the picture is the *Lindley Special*. Lindley is the driver in white shirt and vest. Notice that the *Lindley Special* seems to dwarf most of the cars in the line-up. The OX-5 engine in a Winton chassis gave him quite an advantage over his competitors, and he was undefeated in a long stretch of races on the beach.

This photo was taken in 1922.

FREAK ACCIDENTS

Photo Courtesy Halifax Historical Society

Here's another one of those ex-Army Air Force lieutenants who bought a Jenny and went barnstorming. Lt. Lynn D. Merrill poses in front of his Jenny just north of the Main Street pier. The Jenny in the background belongs to Frank Stanton.

On February 7, 1921, a 19-year-old boy was caught in an undertow just south of the Main Street pier and swept to sea. Pilot Merrill responded to the outcry and immediately took off with passenger Archie Kass, intending to fly low over the drowning youth so that Kass could drop a life preserver. But as Merrill banked over the boy, a wing tip caught a wave and the Jenny cartwheeled into the ocean. Miraculously, neither man was hurt.

Other rescuers pulled the unconscious youth to the slowly sinking wreckage. Meanwhile, pilots Bill Lindley and Stuart Davies had prudently decided to forsake their natural element and launched a rowboat into the surf. They managed to bring all parties to shore and lifeguards were able to revive the boy.

Merrill's wrecked airplane as it appeared after it was dragged out of the surf.

MERRILLS WRECKED PLANE.
RESCUING A DROWNING
PLANE FELL IN OCEAN.

COURSEN PHOTO

Photo Courtesy Halifax Historical Society

Photographer: William L. Coursen

Thus, the story ended happily except for one totally smashed airplane! The public was so taken with Merrill's valiant effort to save the youth that several drives were launched to raise money for a new airplane. March 2, 1921, was declared "Merrill Flight Day" on the beach. Percy Spencer offered his *Lenox* airplane with Harry Copland as pilot for passenger rides, with all proceeds above costs to go into a Merrill fund. Over $2,000 was raised and Merrill had his new airplane shortly thereafter.

Ironically, it was all to no avail. Six months later, on September 1, 1921, while flying his replacement airplane at Lake Winona, Indiana, Merrill went into a dive and never recovered, plunging 2,000 feet to his death.

Bill Lindley experienced this unscheduled dunking while flying passengers off the beach. The ever-enterprising Charles Grenell, who had his photo shop just behind the beach, responded to the hue and cry by grabbing his camera and rushing to the pier. He snapped this photograph and made it into a popular post card.

Photo Courtesy Halifax Historical Society   Photographer: Charles Grenell

On May 6, 1922, Bill Lindley took off in his Jenny northward toward the Main Street fishing pier. His passenger was Mrs. C. W. Adams, wife of a prominent dentist from Detroit, Michigan. As Lindley attempted to gain altitude, his engine lost power and he was unable to rise above the pier. At the last moment he banked toward the ocean, intending to circumvent the pier. But just as he banked, the engine quit completely and he was forced to pancake into the ocean.

Mrs. Adams was unperturbed during the whole adventure, and as the airplane bobbed in the ocean swells, she calmly kept her seat, awaiting the captain's orders to abandon ship!

Believe it or not, little or no damage was done to the plane until it was pulled ashore through the waves. The stress of the pulling snapped the fuselage just behind the pilot's cockpit.

As for Mrs. Adams, such coolness under fire could not go unrewarded. She got to keep her borrowed helmet and goggles as a souvenir!

Another Grenell post card, showing Lindley's wreck just after it was pulled out of the surf.

Photo Courtesy Vivian Robinson

Photographer: Charles Grenell

Almost immediately after the wreck various citizens started a fund to help Lindley replace his airplane. A rope fence was erected around the wreck to keep souvenir hunters at bay until 3:00 p.m. the next day. At that time a memorial service was held over the wrecked plane and pieces of the airplane were sold as part of the fund raising efforts! It must have been successful, because Lindley was soon flying on the beach with a new Jenny.

Photo Courtesy Barbara Lindley Mason

Photographer: Charles Grenell

Photo Courtesy Halifax Historical Society

This is Lindley's Waco 10 in an awkward position just after his *third* engine failure during takeoff! Although the airplane was badly damaged, Lindley completely rebuilt it.

Flying accidents on the beach continued into the late twenties. In May 1928 an inventor named George R. White had constructed an ornithopter airplane (a heavier-than-air machine propelled by flapping wings) and was about to make a test flight from the beach at St. Augustine on May 12. Bill Lindley decided to fly two passengers to St. Augustine to witness the event. On takeoff he encountered crosswinds just as his OX-5 engine lost power. Lindley's Waco sideslipped into the edge of the surf and cartwheeled twice before coming to rest upside down. Incredibly, Lindley walked away unhurt. His two passengers, Murray Cribb from Americus, Georgia, and Pete Craig, local newspaperman and student pilot, suffered minor injuries.

Here is the weird bird that Lindley and his pals didn't get to see. As it turned out, they didn't miss much. There was no test flight of George White's odd aircraft until early summer. Finally on June 16, 1928, with White at the controls, the wing-flapping, foot-propelled ornithopter also crashed on takeoff! White was unhurt.

Photo Courtesy St. Augustine Historical Society

This snapshot illustrates an ever-present hazard in a pilot's life. An inscription on the back of the photo written by Bill Lindley's mother says, "This eagle flew into Bill's Waco plane and was killed. Bill felt so bad about it."

Photo Courtesy Vivian Robinson

LAZY BIRDS

Airplanes were usually shipped to and from the beach by rail during the teens and the early twenties. This unidentified Jenny is probably being put together for the season.

Photographer: Spencer Punnett

The beach had much to offer in the early twenties. You could swim; you could drive; you could fish; you could ride horseback; you could fly — all on the same real estate. Or you could just gather around and talk while you made up your mind! Bill Lindley is on the right of the group of men standing in front of the wing.

Photo Courtesy Barbara Lindley Mason

WATER BIRDS

Photo Courtesy Halifax Historical Society

We haven't said much about tides, but this old snapshot taken by a barefooted (we hope) photographer shows what can happen when a pilot parks his airplane on the beach and wanders off. The unidentified Jenny is just getting its toes wet, but unless a rescue effort is quickly mounted, the wheels will tend to sink. There was probably no real problem here because the airplane was parked high on the beach and only needed to be rolled back a few feet above the high tide mark.

Photo Courtesy Halifax Historical Society

The real tidal problem arrives when an airplane is parked low on the beach. The incoming tide has a chance to engulf both the landing gear and the tail, making the plane hard to move. That's what happened to these two unidentified airplanes. One such incident on December 2, 1925, caught three airplanes and swept them out to sea! Rescuers finally managed to haul them back to shore, but the damage was almost total.

Photo Courtesy Barbara Lindley Mason

Photo Courtesy Halifax Historical Society

Engine trouble forced this seaplane to pay an unscheduled visit to the beach.

What happened to the seaplane pictured here was even worse than the immersions on the preceding page. The seaplane had been taking up passengers from the Halifax River when on March 5, 1921, it encountered engine trouble and was forced to land on the ocean just off the beach.

There were two pilots on board, Fox and Connelly, and one small boy. The pilots taxied the seaplane through the breakers and onto the beach, where they landed the passenger.

As the photograph shows, the two fliers went to work on the engine, and by the next day had it running smoothly. The seaplane was launched into the breakers just when the seas were running a little high. Nevertheless, the two pilots taxied out to about the end of the fishing pier. At that point one especially large wave swamped the aircraft and tore away the lower wings.

Fox immediately abandoned ship and made for shore, but Connelly remained in the cockpit. The seaplane slowly sank, forcing Connelly to perch on the upper wing and watch helplessly as the tide and waves pushed the airplane onto the shore.

Perhaps out of compassion, newspaper accounts never identified which pilot was doing the actual piloting during the entire incident. Maybe it was just as well, since the airplane was almost a total loss.

The only item salvaged from the wreck was the engine. It's hard to imagine another airport that would experience both landplane and seaplane debacles!

FLYING VISITORS

If you couldn't afford a surplus Jenny airplane, you could always build your own. Here's an authentic home-built airplane designed and constructed by Joseph "Jay" Tillis, Jr., of DeLand, Florida. Notice the wee engine perched on the nose of this little sportster. It was a twin-cylinder Indian motorcycle engine putting out 20 hp, specially adapted for Tillis by the Indian Motorcycle Company. Look closely and you'll see a small oil tank on the top wing behind the engine.

Photo Courtesy Halifax Historical Society

Jay Tillis, Jr., creator of the mini-airplane pictured above, learned to fly in a "Canuck" Jenny on Daytona Beach in February 1918, his instructor being Bill Lindley. In those days DeLand had no airport; so the only place Jay could test fly his creation was at Daytona Beach. On August 30, 1921, he brought the above craft over to the beach and parked it on the sand, intending to fly it the next day. He spent the night at a nearby apartment. Unknown to Jay a storm blew up during the evening, and the next morning when he came out, his plane was gone! Frantically searching up and down the beach, he finally found it back in the dunes. There it sat, teetering on its wheels and tail skid, completely intact!

Not that this narrow escape from disaster made much difference. Later in the day Jay got the plane going down the beach, but all it did was hop along like a kangaroo, vibrating badly all the way — a true puddle jumper!

Jay figured that a more powerful engine was needed to get permanently airborne, but his father had other ideas. Ol' dad simply bribed his son to forget the whole thing. History doesn't record what the bribe was, but Jay Tillis' son, still living in DeLand, suspects it might have been a new car. At any rate, Jay Tillis, Jr., scrapped his plane and became a banker.

A Hun in the sun! This genuine German relic of World War I visited the beach briefly in 1921.

Photo Courtesy Halifax Historical Society

The insignia on this airplane is not bogus. It is a genuine World War I German aircraft known as an L.V.G. (Luft-Ver-kehrs-Gesellschaft), and when it landed at Daytona Beach on December 16, 1921, it still had its original camouflage paint! The United States government brought it to this country for evaluation purposes, but they must have sold it as surplus after the war.

The pilot who brought it to Daytona was Walter J. Carr, formerly connected with the Government Aviation Service at Dayton, Ohio. Carr was on the last lap of a flight from Dayton to Miami, where he intended to make his living in commercial aviation.

For its day, the L.V.G. was no slouch. It had a 290-hp Benz engine and was capable of 140 miles per hour. It also must have been a real attention getter. But what did Carr do for spare parts? One can't help but wonder what became of it.

Daytona's beach airport had one unique characteristic not shared by any other airport. It expanded and contracted with the tides. With no hangar in the first line of dunes, pilots usually tucked their airplanes back in the dunes for the night. Here is a visiting Standard aircraft being pulled off the beach. Lettering on the tail identifies the pilot as Lyle Harvey Scott. The smaller lettering indicates that he is proud of his status as an ex-Army pilot, and also proud of his Early Bird license number 309!

Photographer: Spencer Punnett

Scott's plane seems to be safely ensconced in the dunes, but it's doubtful that Scott, in typical barnstorming fashion, unrolled blankets and slept under the wings at night. Sand fleas and blowing sand probably precluded such a life style!

Photographer: Spencer Punnett

The scarcity of airports in Florida decreed that Daytona would be a magnet for visiting pilots, and all sorts of aircraft visited during the twenties. The Martin Bomber above is parked on Ormond Beach around 1923. Just behind the fuselage is the Ormond Golf Course Clubhouse. To the left of the clubhouse is the old Coquina Hotel. Pictures showing aircraft parked as far north as Ormond are rare. The pilot must have been a golfer!

To the left is another view of the Martin Bomber, this time parked next to Bill Lindley's Jenny near the Main Street ocean pier.

THE STUNTMEN

Photo Courtesy Barbara Lindley Mason

Photographer: William L. Coursen

Look, ma, no hands! Pilot Stuart Davies and stuntman-mechanic Lynn Walker engage in some dangerous high jinks.

This is a good illustration of why regulations eventually took a firm grip on pilots. Even in the twenties people were beginning to complain about low flying in populated areas. On this occasion on January 1, 1921, pilot Stuart Davies and stuntman Lynn Walker put on an impromptu show at the request of local photographer W.L. Coursen.

With Coursen aiming his camera from the fishing pier, Davies brought the plane down the beach with the control stick between his knees and his arms extended above his head. Lynn Walker, apparently expressing an abundance of confidence in his pilot, stood on the engine just behind the whirling propeller, leaned back against the upper wing, and extended his arms wide.

Judging by the airplane's shadow on the sand, all this was happening not more than 30 or 35 feet above highly vulnerable motorists and bathers!

Inspired by the numerous automobile speed trials held on the long straightaway beach, Walker and Davies attempted a speed record of their own. With the assistance of race car driver Ralph Mulford in his *Paige 666* stock car, they decided to execute the transfer from car to airplane faster than ever attempted before. On January 4, 1921, they succeeded in establishing a transfer record of 80 miles per hour. Photographer W.L. Coursen was on hand to catch Walker in a frog-like posture just after the exchange.

Here are the highly pleased duo. Pilot Stuart Davies is on the left and stuntman Lynn Walker on the right.

Photo Courtesy Halifax Historical Society

Photographer: William L. Coursen

Photo Courtesy Florida State Archives Photographic Collection

Photo Courtesy Florida State Archives Photographic Collection

At least four flying circuses visited Daytona Beach during 1919 and the 1920's, the Carlstrom Field Flying Circus, the Wrigley Flying Circus, the Mabel Cody Flying Circus, and the Gates Flying Circus. The local boys, particularly Bill Lindley, often put on weekend shows, usually in conjunction with auto races.

The beach, being one long straightaway, was ideal for the transfer stunt shown here. The man making the transfer is acrobat-pilot "Bugs" McGowan. This was a combination practice and camera session on Daytona Beach either in late November or December 1, 1921, prior to a Mabel Cody show at St. Augustine Beach in December.

That it was a photographic session is evident when you notice that the *Miller 8 Special* race car, driven by Sig Haughdahl, is running in the edge of the surf in order to give the photographer in the chase car enough room for a full shot including both plane and car. These photos were used in press releases and on Mabel Cody Circus stationery.

Note Mabel Cody's first name is misspelled on the fuselage. Obviously the lettering man was unsupervised!

In the three photographs on these facing pages, stuntman "Bugs" McGowan executes one of the most popular flying stunts, the transfer of a man from a racing car to an airplane.

Photo Courtesy Florida State Archives Photographic Collection

NIGHT
FLYING

WING
WALKING

AUTO
TO
PLANE
WITH
AND
WITHOUT
LADDER

SINGLE
AND
DOUBLE
PARACHUTE
DROP

STANDING
ON
TOP
OF
PLANE
WHILE
LOOP
THE
LOOP

CHANGING
PLANES
WITHOUT
LADDER

Lt. McGowan
Better Known as
"Bugs McGowan"
General Manager

Mabel Cody
Niece to Buffalo Bill

Richard C. Burns
Director

"Bugs McGowan"

MABEL CODY FLYING CIRCUS
IN THE
WORLDS' GREATEST ATTRACTIONS

Fair Secretaries Wire for Open Dates

Photo Courtesy Barbara Lindley Mason

The Mabel Cody Flying Circus stationery shown here is a kind of summary of the promotional antics of Richard "Curly" Burns, one of the most famous flying circus promoters of the twenties. The Mabel Cody Flying Circus performed at least twice on Daytona Beach featuring Curly's wife Mabel Cody.

Note the reference to Mabel Cody as "niece to Buffalo Bill." This example of Curly's runaway imagination is flatly denied by the International Cody Family Association, which has a list of all descendants of William Cody's immediate family.

The "Lt." McGowan listed at the top of the stationery was personally promoted to that rank by Curly himself. According to "Bugs" McGowan's brother and sister, who were interviewed by the authors in 1988, "Bugs" served in the Army Air Force in World War I but never rose above the rank of private. To his credit he learned to fly informally through his friendships with Army pilots, and during his career as a stuntman he often flew Jennies as part of the flying circus routines.

An unintended double-entendre occurred when someone wrote the bottom line, "Fair Secretaries Wire for Open Dates"!

In 1924 the Mabel Cody Flying Circus came to Daytona Beach to perform there for the first time. On January 7 pilot Russell Holderman took stuntman Billy West aloft to execute a parachute jump before a large crowd of spectators.

As Holderman circled to make his approach run over the beach, West climbed out onto the wing. Suddenly the airplane hit an air pocket and dropped two hundred feet before Holderman could check the fall. West was catapulted from the wing at about 500 feet altitude.

As he fell in a long arch toward the beach, the horrified crowd could see that his parachute canopy had failed to open. It simply trailed behind Billy like a fluttering ribbon as he plunged downward.

With an audible thud, West hit the soft sand of the upper beach. Bystanders rushed to his inert form, certain that he was dead — but much to everyone's amazement he was still alive! He had serious injuries, but after three months in a hospital he recovered completely.

Later, when interviewed about his experience, West remembered his plunge vividly. The usual idea that a man's whole life flashes before him as he faces certain death didn't seem to apply to West. "I was conscious all the way down," he said, "and all the time I was thinking some mighty hard thoughts about that company that made my parachute!"

One good thing about surviving a 500-foot fall is that you can sue the parachute company — and Billy West did! Shortly thereafter West returned to stunt work as if nothing had happened.

During a long lull between stunt engagements he had to seek another line of work; so he returned to Daytona Beach and became a motorcycle cop.

Less than a week after beginning his new job, a Ford smashed into his motorcycle at an intersection. West was knocked unconscious and dragged twenty feet.

This time he was only slightly injured, but nevertheless that was enough. To everyone's surprise he promptly turned in his badge and announced that he was returning to the less hazardous work of a flying stuntman!

Photo Courtesy Embry-Riddle Aeronautical University

Billy West poses several years after his dramatic plunge described on this page. "Billy West" was a show biz name. His real name was Irwin R. Westheimer. After years of stunt work, he learned to fly in 1929 so that he could add the stunt of crashing an airplane to his repertoire.

Most famous of all the touring flying shows was the Gates Flying Circus. They performed on Daytona Beach at least twice in the 1920's, in 1926 and 1927. In spite of the daring stunts illustrated in their advertisement on this page, the secret of their success was their emphasis on passenger rides. They flew Standard J-1's with Hisso engines (superior to the Jenny and its unreliable OX-5 engine) and enlarged the front cockpit to hold four passengers — two pairs facing each other. Steel ladders were permanently bolted on both sides of the passenger cockpit. After a ride passengers could be quickly disembarked on one side while new passengers were being loaded on the other!

Promoter Ivan Gates was efficient in other ways, too. When his number one wingwalker was killed in a flying accident, Gates found himself stuck with thousands of advertising posters bearing the wingwalker's name. To curb such waste in the future, Gates devised the name "Diavalo" to designate his No. 1 wingwalker, a name that could be transferred to the next wingwalker in case of a fatal accident. At the time af the advertisement shown here, his main wingwalker had proven to be so daring and indestructable that Gates risked billing him as "Diavalo" A.F. Frantz, a tribute even though wingwalker A.F. Krantz got his name misspelled!

Photo Courtesy Embry-Riddle Aeronautical University

This group of pilots and stuntmen were photographed in front of a Curtiss Oriole during the Aero-Auto Meet held in Daytona Beach on March 29 through April 2, 1922. Standing left to right are Bill Lindley (in his typical pose), Glenn E. Messer (pilot and stuntman), Steve Crane (pilot and owner of the Curtiss Oriole), Gustav "Slim" Ekstrom (pilot). Front row, left to right are Jimmy Johnson (pilot), Joe Wilson (stuntman), and Joe Nichols (pilot and stuntman).

Photo Courtesy Barbara Lindley Mason

Bill Lindley and Gustav Ekstrom are discussed elsewhere in this book. Steve Crane, at the time the photograph was taken, was living in Pablo Beach, Jacksonville.

Jimmy Johnson went with three different airlines after his barnstorming days. First he joined Chalk Airlines in Miami (oldest continuously operating flying service in the world, and still operating scheduled flights to the Bahamas today), then he went with Orlando Airlines, and finally he became a chief pilot with United Airlines. The fate of Joe Wilson and Joe Nichols is unknown.

Glenn Messer and Gustav are members of the fabled The Early Birds of Aviation, Inc., an organization conceived in 1928, whose members soloed either a balloon, airship, glider or airplane before December 17, 1916. That date was chosen as the cutoff date denoting pioneer pilots because it was the thirteenth anniversary of the Wrights' flight and the date on which the Government began financing pilot training in preparation for World War I.

Gustav Ekstrom died on July 7, 1968, in Coral Gables, Florida, but Glenn Messer is still living. Glenn learned to fly a Wright Model B in 1911 when he was only 16 years old. Soon after soloing Messer was flying exhibitions on weekends while still going to school! During World War I he flew in the Royal Flying Corps. In the twenties he returned to exhibition flying and organized the Messer Flying Circus. Besides doing flying and stunt work himself, he had as many as 28 men in his circus, with different units putting on shows nationwide.

Messer appears in the picture on the previous page because he had been brought to Daytona to organize what was to be the largest auto-aerial regatta ever staged in Florida. He was also hired to do daredevil airplane stunts and one stunt in particular that had nothing to do with airplanes at all.

Being a big strong fellow, he had devised an act where he braced himself in a moving truck and pulled five cars in tandem behind by holding the towing rope in his mouth by means of a specially constructed mouth piece. Ordinarily Messer had his own driver to drive the towing truck, as the pull had to be gentle and slow in *low gear only*. The local sponsor of the stunt was Green Brothers Dodge Motor Company. One of the Green boys wanted to get into the act and insisted on driving the tow truck. Naturally he was given careful instructions about staying in low gear.

Everything started off nicely and was moving so well that Green decided to go faster — and shifted gears! The resulting jerk snapped the mouth piece out of Messer's mouth, forcing his upper and lower foreteeth horizontal, and broke his jaw! He was immediately rushed to the dental office of Bill Lindley's father-in-law, where his teeth and jaw were wired back into position. About six weeks later he was posing for the picture on the previous page, complete with original teeth!

The man in white atop the upper wing is the fully recovered Glenn Messer ready to perform stunts during the Aero-Auto Meet held on March 29-April 2, 1922. The pilot is Bill Lindley, flying his own Jenny. Messer is wearing a white headband to keep his hair from whipping his face while in flight.

Photo Courtesy Halifax Historical Society

In the photograph above, Glenn Messer is about to stand atop the wing while Lindley takes off and performs a loop. As you can see, Messer performed this stunt without a parachute.

Although most stuntmen performed the loop stunt wearing a harness hooked to wires attached to the upper wing, Messer did not like a harness because it prevented him from leaning into the wind. So he dispensed with the harness and put both feet into metal stirrups attached to the upper wing. The left stirrup had a strap attached which held the foot securely in the stirrup, but the right stirrup was arranged so his right foot could be moved in or out.

This worked all right at Daytona, but a year later when Messer performed this stunt in Alabama, the left footstrap broke when the airplane was upside down at the top of the loop. Messer was blown back off the top wing and as the plane continued in its loop, he struck the fuselage atop the pilot

Sidney Molloy. Evidently possessed of fabulous reflexes, Molloy grabbed Messer and managed to pull him into the cockpit while at the same time completing the loop!

Messer was knocked unconscious during the mishap and did not regain consciousness until the aircraft landed. Fortunately he was not hurt and continued to operate his flying circus and perform all his stunts as if nothing had happened. The hair-raising incident was later recorded in the John Hix syndicated feature, *Strange As It Seems*.

Glenn Messer is a survivor in more ways than one. At this writing (March 1990) he is one of ten Early Bird pilots still living. Now 95, he is in the *Guinness Book of Records*, having flown as a pilot in powered flight more consecutive years than anyone in the world. Beginning in 1911, he flew continuously until 1982, a total of 71 years!

By 1923 Louis "Bugs" McGowan had left the Mabel Cody Flying Circus and was a free-lance pilot and stuntman. Here he is in front of Bill Lindley's *Rio Vista* Jenny in January 1923.

According to Early Bird pilot Glenn Messer, the vertical exhaust pipes shown in this photograph are not a special modification by Bill Lindley. That's the way they were originally installed. Messer should know. He bought 52 Jennies from the Government just after World War I for $52.12 apiece for resale to civilians.

Photo Courtesy Edward McGowan

Photo Courtesy Birthplace of Speed Museum

Glenn Messer once described Bill Lindley as the ideal pilot for a stuntman — skillful, steady, and *very* careful! In this dramatic scene Lindley is slowly bringing his right wing skid forward into position for "Bugs" McGowan to execute the transfer from car to plane. Note the exhaust pipes were modified by Lindley to emit the exhaust alongside the fuselage.

McGowan and Lindley performed together in at least three flying shows on the beach during January 1923.

About six months after this picture was taken, McGowan put on a stunt show at the Isle of Palms, South Carolina, on July 4. As a grand finale, he went aloft alone to perform a stunt he had never attempted before. Carrying a can of gasoline, he intended to set the airplane on fire and parachute to safety. But something went wrong. Probably in the thinner air of the higher altitude the gas can expanded and exploded. The Jenny was seen to nose over and dive, trailing a long plume of smoke. As his young wife watched in mounting horror, the plane and pilot plunged 1,500 feet into the sea.

An autopsy revealed that "Bugs" died from smoke inhalation. He was only 21 years old.

In this photo post card "Bugs" McGowan hangs from the lower wing of Lindley's *Rio Vista* Jenny. Grenell got it all wrong describing McGowan as hanging from a wing skid.

Photo Courtesy Barbara Lindley Mason

Photographer: Charles Grenell

COWAN'S BEACH AIRPORT

Daytona Beach rumrunner "Red" Cowan built this shack on the beach as his refueling station for aircraft.

Photo Courtesy *The News-Journal* Library

In 1924 a new type of pilot joined aviation on the beach — the rumrunner. Ever since the Volstead Act of 1919 banning the sale of intoxicating beverages in the United States, Daytona Beach had experienced more than its share of rumrunning. The south end of the beach at the inlet was the main point of entry for fast speedboats carrying whisky for unloading at local wharfs.

Daytona's number one rumrunner was Winder "Red" Cowan, and in 1924 he built a shack on the beach several miles south of the Main Street pier. All during the middle and late twenties Red operated it as a refueling station for aircraft using the beach, but it gradually became known as a "refueling" station for pilots too — or anyone else who happened to have a dry palate. For years it was called Red's Place, although local papers more circumspectly referred to it as "Cowan's Beach Airport."

Cowan himself was a pilot and owned several planes during the twenties. In particular, he owned a Standard with a Hisso engine and employed a professional pilot, Charles Wetheren, to fly it. Officially the Standard was used to offer passenger rides and flight instruction, but unofficially Cowan put the reliable Hisso engine to more profitable use transporting cases of whisky. In typical pirate fashion, this booty was often buried in the dunes behind Red's Place. How could "Red" operate with such impunity? Well, for one thing, from 1921 to 1927 he was a Daytona Beach motorcycle cop!

Cowan had taken the trouble to build Red's Place on pilings so that exceptionally high tides would merely wash underneath. All was well until a big storm hit in 1932. "It was built so strong it didn't come apart," Red said in an interview many years later. "It just floated away like a houseboat."

Photo Courtesy Barbara Lindley Mason

Photographer: Richard H. LeSesne

This aerial view of "Cowan's Beach Airport" was taken by photographer Richard LeSesne, who unfortunately took his picture at high tide when most of the runway was under water. However, this scene taken during the winter of 1928 gives a good impression of the isolation of Cowan's refueling station several miles south of the Main Street pier.

An arrow points to Red's Place sitting on the dividing line between the beach and dunes. Directly to the left of the arrow is the house that Cowan rented. Bill Lindley's two-story house is a few feet north of the rented house. One can just make out Lindley's airplane parked in the dunes in front of his house.

Behind these properties, running north and south the length of the beach, is South Atlantic Boulevard. To the west is the still existent Lindley Road, which was named after Bill Lindley, and on which his daughter Barbara Sue Mason still lives.

Bill Lindley greets one of the genuine celebrities of the 1920's, pilot Clarence Chamberlin.

Photo Courtesy Barbara Lindley Mason

It's difficult for anyone born after World War II to realize how famous the record setting pilots were in the years leading up to World War II. Lindbergh, for instance, was such a great hero that President Franklin Roosevelt feared him as a possible rival in a presidential race.

The man climbing out of the little biplane shown here wasn't quite that famous, but he was a genuine celebrity nevertheless. He was Clarence Chamberlin, and he had just landed at Cowan's Beach Airport on the afternoon of February 21, 1928, enroute to a Tampa air show. Almost seven months earlier — two weeks after Lindbergh landed in Paris — Chamberlin took off from New York in a Wright Bellanca named *Miss Columbia* and headed for Berlin, Germany. His sponsor Charles A. Levine accompanied him as passenger. Chamberlin ran short of fuel and landed 100 miles short of Berlin in Eiselben, Germany. Thus he was the first pilot to carry a passenger across the Atlantic Ocean, setting a world's nonstop distance record of 3,911 miles. When he landed at Daytona Beach, he was flying a sport plane known as a Sperry Messenger.

Here's another view of Chamberlin's Sperry Messenger parked next to Cowan's shack. Note the refueling drums in the background. Also note the rope to ward off the curious. The Sperry Messenger was considered an outstanding design in its time, even though only 32 were built. One example still exists today on loan to the Air Force Museum at Wright-Patterson AFB, Dayton, Ohio.

Photo Courtesy Barbara Lindley Mason

This snapshot, taken in the late twenties in front of Cowan's shack, is something of a mystery. What's the Laird Speedwing mail plane normally found on the Chicago-Minneapolis-St. Paul route doing here so far from home? Note the three airplanes hauled up in the dunes behind and to the right of Cowan's operation shack, better known as Red's Place. The house in the background belonged to Bill Lindley's father-in-law, Dr. William W. Wilder. Cowan rented it for a residence and undoubtedly used it for "storage," too.

Photographer: Spencer Punnett

FLYING VISITORS: BIGGER AND BETTER

Photo Courtesy John Gontner

The ocean hopping *Pride of Detroit* arrives at the beach. Local photographer Richard LeSesne is seen on the right operating a movie camera. The two helmeted pilots standing at the left are unidentified. On the far left the bare-headed man is the author's uncle, pilot Spencer Punnett, who often flew off the beach during the twenties and thirties.

Later in the twenties, as the war surplus airplanes began to wear out or become obsolete, advanced airplanes began to appear with the more powerful and reliable radial engines. The photograph above heralds the arrival in December 1927 of a nationally famous flying team, Ed Schlee and Bill Brock, in their famous Stinson aircraft *Pride of Detroit*.

Schlee was a wealthy businessman and owner of the airplane. Brock was his pilot. They had just made an audacious attempt to fly around the world only weeks after Lindbergh's

conquest of the Atlantic. They flew the Atlantic, continued eastward over Europe and Asia to Japan, and were poised to conquer the Pacific when sustained bad weather forced them to abandon the rest of the flight.

Still seeking new worlds to conquer, Schlee and Brock came to Daytona Beach in an attempt to establish a world's endurance record. The record at that time was 28 days, 14 hours and 36 minutes. Problems developed, and they decided to abandon the attempt.

Edward Schlee and William Brock stand in front of the *Pride of Detroit*. Schlee is dressed in white. The rotund Brock, among all the famous record-setting pilots of the 1920's, clearly wins the prize as the least likely looking glamorous, dashing pilot!

Photo Courtesy Halifax Historical Society

Bill Brock was one of the most illustrious of the Early Bird pilots who visited the beach. As a youngster attending school in Springfield, Ohio, he was inspired by the exploits of Lincoln Beachey and other barnstorming pilots who toured the country around 1912.

Determined to become a pilot himself, Brock quit school at the age of 16. Without telling his parents of his aspirations, he went to Ithaca, New York, and got a job with the Thomas Aircraft Company, which was then turning out the Thomas pusher airplane. He negotiated a deal to work for seventy-six consecutive weeks for seven dollars a week plus flying lessons.

In three months Brock was assistant instructor and in seven was chief test pilot!

In 1916 he left the company with his own Thomas pusher to become an exhibition pilot, and his first contract brought him back to Springfield. Word spread that the local high school dropout had made good, and the entire population turned out at the county fair "to see Billy go up in an airplane."

Like so many of the Early Bird pilots, Brock was an instructor during World War I, and then became a barnstormer and air-mail pilot before joining up with wealthy oilman Ed Schlee. Brock died of illness in 1932 at the age of 36.

According to the lettering on this Stinson Detroiter monoplane, somebody from the Oklahoma Aero Club visited the beach in 1929. This same aircraft, registered NC 1929, was Braniff Airline's first airplane when Braniff was the Tulsa-Oklahoma City Airline. The airplane began operations on June 20, 1928, flying three round trips daily. How it happened to be visiting Daytona Beach is anyone's guess!

Photo Courtesy Halifax Historical Society

In February 1929 the Army Air Force sent some aircraft on a 12,000-mile goodwill tour of South America. Here is one of the aircraft, a Keystone Loening amphibian, during a stopover on Daytona Beach.

Photographer: Spencer Punnett

Photo Courtesy Halifax Historical Society

A rare bird makes its appearance on the beach — the single boom Sikorsky S-36 amphibian.

This Sikorsky amphibian didn't land on the beach even though you see it parked on the sand just in front of the Clarendon Hotel. On March 20, 1928, it landed on the ocean just outside the breakers, calmly lowered its landing wheels, and taxied in through the surf and onto the beach right in front of the Hotel, probably causing a mild sensation in the process!

Pilot C.B.D. Collyer and mechanic John Johannson then took dinner at the Clarendon and stayed the night, thereby pointing out another unique feature of a beach airport.

This Sikorsky S-36 was leased by Pan American Airways, Inc., from the Sikorsky Company and used to test the theory of operating in the Caribbean with amphibious, instead of land, aircraft. When Collyer landed at Daytona, he was in the process of returning from that assignment. Only five S-36 amphibian aircraft were built; so pictures like this one are not common. Sadly, in November of that same year, while attempting a transcontinental speed record, Collyer crashed into a canyon wall in Arizona and was killed.

Photo Courtesy Halifax Historical Society

Photographer: Richard H. LeSesne

Yes, the sand was hard enough to accommodate the big boys, too! This is the Royal Typewriter Company's Ford tri-motor plane visiting Daytona Beach in 1927.

END OF AN ERA

As the twenties drew to a close, it was clear that times were changing. There was an increased use of the beach by automobiles, pushing flying activity further south, and Daytona Beach wanted an airport that would attract airlines without worrying about cars or tides. So the City built its first inland airport on Bethune Point along the west bank of the Halifax River. In response to this facility, the federal government inaugurated the first Air Mail Service from Daytona Beach on March 1, 1929. None other than hometown Ervie Ballough was to make that first flight from Bethune Point. After all, it was a family tradition.

Fifty years earlier, when Daytona was a tiny settlement on the Halifax River, Ervie's uncle Charles Ballough, with a mule-driven gig, had inaugurated a new mail service when he brought the mail over the Old King's Highway from St. Augustine to Daytona. On every trip he was armed to the teeth. Indians were no longer a threat, but highwaymen, snakes and alligators were!

Unfortunately this family tradition died when a last-minute injury forced Ervie Ballough to withdraw from piloting the inaugural flight.

Here is Ballough's substitute, pilot C. James Faulkner, about to takeoff from Bethune Point in a Pitcairn Mailwing. His cargo was eight bags of mail bound for Orlando and Tampa. He took off and promptly crashed in the Halifax River!

Photo Courtesy Halifax Historical Society

This is what was left of the Pitcairn Mailwing when salvage operations got underway. The mail was fished out intact and pilot Faulkner escaped with nothing worse than a cut nose!

Photo Courtesy Halifax Historical Society

Several Daytona Beach investors joined with Bill Lindley to form Florida State Airways, Inc., intending to establish a scheduled passenger and air freight business on the Florida east coast. Lindley is shown on the left about to take off from the beach in the company flagship sometime in late December 1929. The comely young lady peering from the cabin window is Vivian Veronica Von Hagen, Bill Lindley's niece. Lindley is flying a new Ryan six-passenger monoplane christened *Miss Daytona Beach.* With its enclosed cabin, Bill's appearance changes. A businesslike snapbrim hat replaces the dashing helmet and goggles!

Photo Courtesy Vivian Robinson

Ironically, aviation on the beach saw its life span essentially bracketed between two crashes — the Charles Hamilton crash in January 1906, to begin flying off the beach, and the Faulkner crash which was the significant symbolic end because it inaugurated the use of the Bethune Point Airport. After the Faulkner crash, a substitute airplane resumed air-mail flights from Bethune Point, and shortly thereafter Eastern Air Transport (a predecessor to Eastern Airlines) began to use the new facility.

In retrospect, beach flying really received a triple blow. First was the new inland airport at Bethune Point; then the stock market crash of October 1929; and finally a third event occurred on January 19, 1930. On that day Bill Lindley took off on the second leg of a chartered flight from the Bahamas to Palm Beach. He was flying *Miss Daytona Beach,* a new Ryan cabin monoplane with pontoons. Four passengers were aboard. As Lindley approached Palm Beach, he circled Lake Worth and started his descent to land. The airplane never pulled out of the dive and plunged into the lake with the engine at full throttle. Lindley and two mechanics were killed instantly.

Testimony from the only survivor indicated that the cause of the crash was mechanical failure. Daytona Beach was shocked at the news. Its most popular local pilot was gone, and with him went the driving force of that bizarre and wonderful era of flying on the beach.

EXTRA

The Sunday News-Journal

EXTRA

VOL. 4—NO. 16   ASSOCIATED PRESS AND INTERNATIONAL ILLUSTRATED NEWS   DAYTONA BEACH, FLORIDA, SUNDAY, JANUARY 19, 1930   MEMBER AUDIT BUREAU OF CIRCULATIONS TELEPHONE 2000   Price, 5c; Sunday, 10c

DAYTONA AIRMEN KILLED!

GILLESPIE IS PRESIDENT OF NEW LEAGUERS

Plans For Work Perfected At Meeting Held Recently

TO OUST DeLAND GANG

By GUS MARTIN
Staff Correspondent

NEW SMYRNA, Jan. 18.—A permanent organization, to be known as the Home Rule League of New Smyrna, was perfected here last night at a meeting of influential citizens. J. U. Gillespie was elected president and L. B. Smith, secretary.

Primary purposes of this organization are: To secure home rule for New Smyrna by supporting candidates who will work for complete separation of city affairs from county politics and DeLand domination; an economical administration which will eliminate the cumbersome and expensive organization now maintained by the city which is now costing at least $20,000 per year more than is necessary in a place of this size; and the election of officers who will at all times take the people into their confidence in all of the conditions of the city including its financial situation.

It is the desire of this organization to enlist as members all citizens who are interested in the general welfare of the city civically, politically and economically. No membership fee are to be charged as the association is working strictly upon a utilitarian basis.

"Miss Daytona Beach" Christened Here Recently

"Miss Daytona Beach No. 1" which made a fatal plunge into Lake Worth today, was flagship of the Florida State Airways, Inc., of Daytona Beach.

The ship was christened December 26 on its arrival at the Daytona Beach airport, piloted by William Lindley from St. Louis. It was a sister-ship to Col. Charles A. Lindbergh's "Spirit of St. Louis," although the most modern ship manufactured by Ryan.

Luxuriously Fitted

A six-place cabin monoplane, "Miss Daytona" was luxuriously outfitted as a limousine and was the first of six ships of the same type to be placed in service by the company.

Interchangeable landing wheels and pontoons were provided and the ship was on pontoons at the time of the crash, just returning from a trip to West End, a Caribbean island.

The Florida State Airways, Inc., was formed a few months ago to engage in passenger and express carrying throughout Florida with Daytona Beach as headquarters.

"Bill" Lindley was vice-president of the corporation. Charles W. Sellick, who earlier formed the Sellick Airways here, is president. Mrs. Fanny Schulnan is treasurer. Joseph Ginsberg, in addition to serving as secretary, represents the company as attorney.

Plans announced by the company a few weeks ago were to cover the state of Florida with every type of air service practicable. For the present, it was announced, a passenger and express service along the entire east coast was to be inaugurated. Until this feature could be scheduled for operation an air taxi service was to have been operated.

TAG DEADLINE IN FORCE HERE

Volusia county motorists will get no extension of time to obtain 1930 license plates, Sheriff S. E. Stone, informed The News-Journal by telephone last night.

A round-up of delinquents will begin tomorrow morning in compliance with the latest information from the state motor vehicle department, the sheriff stated. He made no provision for those who violate the law today.

Constable George L. Haney will act likewise here in compliance with orders from Tallahassee.

It's Different Elsewhere

Great disparity in enforcement

LICENSE GIVES POLICE CLEW

JACKSONVILLE, Jan. 18.—(AP)—A Massachusetts license tag or a stolen automobile led today to identification of two of three bandits who last night shot and seriously wounded two city detectives in a pistol battle.

A local man, whose name police refused to divulge, identified from photographs Roland Lalone and Watson Moulthrope, two escaped convicts from Wethersfield state prison, Connecticut. The third man was believed to be Leo Landry who escaped with Lalone and Moul-

AT CONTROLS OF ILL-FATED PLANE

'Bill' Lindley, Pilot, Dies in Plane Crash At W. Palm Beach

Two Local Mechanics Also Perish; Two Passengers Are Dying; Plane Plunges Into Lake Worth

DROWNED; PINNED IN WRECK

Special to The News-Journal

WEST PALM BEACH, Jan. 19.—William Lindley, Edwin Omps and Al Lipsky, all of Daytona Beach, were instantly killed in an airplane crash here this afternoon.

Two other passengers in the plane piloted by Lindley, which plunged into Lake Worth shortly after 3 o'clock, were badly wounded and rushed to a local hospital where they are not expected to live. They were Edward S. Butler of Miami and Elbert Stassel of West Gates, a suburb of Palm Beach.

Flew "Miss Daytona Beach"

The men were occupants of a Ryan cabin monoplane, "Miss Daytona Beach," owned by the Florida State Airways, Inc., of Daytona Beach, and were attempting to make a landing here when the plane suddenly dived into the lake.

The three men from Daytona Beach were instantly killed or drowned while pinned in the wreckage. One of the bodies is still pinned in the wreckage and will not be removed tonight.

The plane, owned by the company, of which Lindley was vice-president.

Witnesses of the accident stated that Lindley circled above the Roosevelt and

Photo Courtesy Vivian Robinson

The era when pilots were heroes! Bill Lindley's death prompted Daytona's local newspaper to run an EXTRA — a form of attention usually reserved for major national events.

BIBLIOGRAPHY

Bowen, Ezra, and the Editors of Time-Life Books. *Knights of the Air.* Time-Life Books, Alexandria, Virginia, 1980.

Boyne, Walter J. *The Aircraft Treasures of Silver Hill.* Rawson Associates, New York, 1982.

Caidin, Martin. *Barnstorming.* Duell, Sloan and Pearce, New York, 1965.

Gardner, Lester D. (compiled by). *Who's Who in American Aeronautics.* Aviation Publishing Corp., New York, 1928.

Gray, "Jack" Stearns. *"Up" A True Story Of Aviation.* Shenandoah Publishing House, Inc., Strasburg, Virginia, 1931.

Harris, Sherwood. *The First to Fly.* Simon & Schuster, New York, 1970.

Jablonski, Edward. *Atlantic Fever.* The MacMillan Co., Inc., New York, 1972.

Jablonski, Edward. *Sea Wings.* Doubleday & Company, Inc., Garden City, New York, 1972.

Lazarus, William C. *Wings In The Sun.* Tyn Cobb's Florida Press, Orlando, Florida, 1951.

Palmer, Henry R. *This Was Air Travel.* Bonanza Books, New York, 1960.

Taylor, Michael J.H. and Mondey, David. *Milestones of Flights.* Jane's Publishing Company, Limited, London, England, 1983.

Vecsey, George and Dade, George C. *Getting Off the Ground.* E.P. Dutton, New York, 1979.

The following newspapers and magazines were used in our research:

Aerial Age Weekly

Aero

Aero & Hydro

Aeronautics — The American Magazine Of Aerial Navigation (New York)

Colliers

The Daytona Daily News

The Daytona Evening News

The Daytona Gazette-News

The Daytona Morning News

The DeLand News

The Florida Times Union

Flying and Aero Club of America Bulletin (New York)

Miami Daily Metropolis

The Observer

St. Augustine Evening Record

Quitman Free Press

Southern Aviation

The Vintage Airplane

United States Air Service

Utica Daily Press

INDEX

ABOUT THE AUTHORS

Do two cooks spoil the broth? Not if they have a clear division of labor. Dick Punnett did research and all the writing for *Thrills, Chills & Spills.* His wife Yvonne thought up the project, found most of the pictures, did an equal share of the research, all the typing, acted as editor, and generally cracked the whip — gently, of course!

This happy cooperation resulted from blending yet diverse careers. Dick grew up in Penfield, New York, and graduated from Principia College in Elsah, Illinois. After further studies at the Art Center School and Chouinard Art Institute in Los Angeles, he became a storyboard man for a Hollywood animation studio. He is the author of eight children's books for pre-school through second grade — the popular *Talk-Along*

educational series and the *Double-Rhyme* series.

Yvonne Punnett grew up in Hollywood, California, and graduated from Principia College in Elsah, Illinois. After graduate school at U.C.L.A., she became a secondary teacher of English and history in both public and private schools for ten years. After a number of years in the business world, serving mainly as a secretary, she became her husband's literary agent in 1980.

As some of the photographs in this book indicate, the Punnetts are ardent collectors of Florida pictorial history, with emphasis on old Florida photographs and stereographs.

The couple now live in Ormond Beach and divide their time between Florida and New York state.